Natu

Edited by Maryam Fanni,
Matilda Flodmark, Sara Kaaman

Occasional Papers

Introduction

The Book as a Pot-Luck Offering: Edna Beilenson, Jane Grabhorn & the Books of the Distaff Side

The Vampire and the Darling Priest of Modernism

A Darn Good Idea: Feminist printers and the Women's Liberation Movement in Britain

Further Reading

Thank You

Facsimile from the book *Bookmaking on the Distaff Side*
"Leisure." Verse from The Poetry Book-
shop of London. Design, woodcut and
hand colouring by Lucina Wakefield.

Colophon

Maryam Fanni, Matilda Flodmark
and Sara Kaaman

This book started with curiosity, and a
wish to trace the (Euro-American) roots
of the professional landscape that a newly
graduated graphic designer is facing
today. We wanted to understand what lies
behind (and before) the professional
identity and working conditions
presented as given, even desirable—that
of the graphic designer as a freelancing
and independent "creative", self-made
and self-hired.

> She now works flexibly from home,
> without external controls. She works
> when she wants to. However, she has
> to carry out an incalculable amount
> of work for a fixed fee. This means that
> she does nothing but work at home.
> The route to the desk to read e-mails
> and answer e-mails at her laptop has
> become as much of a routine as the way
> to the kitchen to make coffee. The jobs
> she is paid for, those done and those not
> done, are only a small part of what she

does every day. Organising a meeting, doing the washing, learning a new programme, preparing dinner, writing invoices, shopping, doing her tax return, booking a flight, keeping up contacts, showing interest—all this becomes too much for her sometimes.

This excerpt from the text "A comment by", written in 2011 by the German artist collective Kleines postfordisches Drama,[1] describes the everyday life of many freelancers. A precarious, tough and in many ways lonely condition. But at the same time framed with apparently positive words like freedom and flexibility.

Throughout our collaboration we have tried to formulate other ways of working. We wanted to trace a professional identity that is built on collectivity, community, and an understanding of material conditions, rather than on individuality and success stories.

The point of departure for this book was the encounter with *Bookmaking on the Distaff Side*, a book published in

San Francisco in 1937, collecting over twenty contributions, many of them experimental, by a diverse group of practitioners working within printing, typography and book production. On page 26 of this book, book historian Kathleen Walkup describes it as "an eclectic mix of articles, poems and tributes that are often humorous and occasionally apologetic [and that] contains several well-researched essays that examine the role women have played in the history of Euro-American trade printing."[2]

Although, almost 80 years separate us from *Bookmaking on the Distaff Side*—laptops and flexible working hours have replaced heavy metal typesetting and the punch clock—we were struck by how contemporary some of the testimonies sound. In her feminist critique of a male-dominated profession, Jane Grabhorn writes about typographers as "pompering, tottering pretenders, mouthing decedit and sweating decadence". We found the book comforting and encouraging as it provided us with a link to a history of women in our professions. In reading the various stories of women working in roles that would later become identified as part of the "graphic design" field, we were able to better understand our own professional identities. We were able to see more clearly how what we do and how we work is a patchwork of tasks and jobs that have shifted with technological and economical changes, and that will keep shifting.

Initially we asked ourselves what a contemporary version of *Bookmaking on the Distaff Side* would look like. What would be the testimonies of women in corresponding professions today?

But such an undertaking—to select a range of contemporary voices that fit neatly into one volume—felt exclusive rather than inclusive. It would risk becoming a manifestation of our own, necessarily limited viewpoint of the "trade" or "field" of graphic design. Often when attempts are made to rewrite history in an effort to make room for women, it is done in the form of searching for and presenting individual success stories. New names are added to the canon. Without downplaying the importance of this strategy, we find that it tends to overshadow anonymous workers and collectives, such as the less glamorous stories of, for example, trade unions. When looking for the histories of collective labour and collegiality that do not result in elevated singular names, another picture of the past emerges, which might in turn help us re-imagine the future.

In search of this picture, we assembled a selection of stories of what happened between 1937 (when *Bookmaking on the Distaff Side* was published) and today (2020). We wanted to understand some of the material working conditions of our female forerunners. What has printing (together) meant to women, both as an engagement for women's rights and in terms of making a living? This book offers a selection of such perspectives on women and printing.

Departing from the 1937 book, Kathleen Walkup and poet Ida Börjel have written on some of the individuals and collaborations involved in that volume. Walkup presents the key figures, among others Edna Beilenson, Jane Grabhorn and Beatrice Warde, and provides a context for the Distaff Side initiative and how *Bookmaking on the Distaff Side*, which she describes as a pot-luck, came about. Börjel's essay starts from Gertrude Stein's involvement, and offers a portrayal of the relationship between Stein and Laura Riding, which revolved around printing, and an Albion hand press in particular. These essays provide examples of women collaborating in order to gain control over print production, in what later became known as the private press movement.

Another example of the necessity of taking control over print production is the emergence of radical printshops in the period between the 1960s and 1980s. Jess Baines, herself an active member of the See Red Women's Workshop, among others, has done extensive research interviewing people who were engaged in such printshops in order to collect and write their histories. Her contribution to the present volume gives an insight into the activities and principles of feminist printshops in London, during the Women's Liberation Movement.

The final text contribution is an excerpt from a book by economic historian Ulla Wikander, in which she offers a historical perspective on the conditions under which women entered the typography trade in the late 1800s and early 1900s, which she describes as a battle between men and women.

This battle took place again during the technological revolution provoked by digitisation in 1970s and 1980s. To shed light on the working conditions as well as the organising and struggles around this time, we have interviewed four women with various experiences in the printing trade. The conversations with Inger Humlesjö and Ingegärd Waaranperä address, respectively, the construction of masculinity and the conditions of being a typesetter during the reorganisations of one of Sweden's biggest newspapers. In Britain we met Gail Cartmail and Megan Dobney, two prominent names in contemporary trade unions, who both were union activists within the printing trades. These conversations refer to the Wapping Dispute of 1986, and the organisation of printers in Britain against South African apartheid, as well as the challenging questions around union strategies in times of technological development.

Our book borrows its title from the contribution of Anne Lyon Haight in *Bookmaking on the Distaff Side*, in which she refers to the book historian William

Blades, who classified women along "with the other enemies of books: damp, dust, dirt, book worms, careless readers, borrowers, book stealers, book-ghouls, etc".[3] Haight writes about the Medieval nun Hrotsvitha and other important female book collectors throughout history. Haight's contribution is illustrated with a wood carving by Anne Heyneman, depicting drunk nuns rumbling around carelessly in a library, which we also chose as the cover image of this book.

Alongside researching for and editing this book, we have experimented hands-on with various graphic and typographic techniques, using *Bookmaking on the Distaff Side* as a source of inspiration. One of the techniques was the making of paste papers, as a tribute to Delight Rushmore, who made unique paste paper covers for each copy of the edition of 100 books. In fact our copy was originally her own—on the inside of the cover we can read "no 37, Delight's copy".

Some of the paste papers that we made collectively can be found throughout this book as chapter dividers. Perusing this book—designed by the designer trio Eller med a—the reader will also come across selected facsimiles, as well as small graphic elements from the original *Bookmaking on the Distaff Side*.

This book is a collage of images, testimonies and personal histories at the intersections of technology, work and life. A "messy history" as opposed to a "neat history", in the words of graphic design historian Martha Scotford.[4] Our ambition is not to be exhaustive on the topic, but rather to contribute to an expanded feminist historiography of contemporary graphic design. We hope you will enjoy it.

1   *Casco Issues XII: Generous Structures*, edited by Binna Choi and Axel Wieder, Utrecht and New York/Berlin: Casco and Sternberg Press, 2011, pp. 49–55.

2   We first came across *Bookmaking on the Distaff Side* via the online exhibition catalogue of *Unseen Hands – Women Printers, Binders & Book Designers* organised by Princeton University Library (2002–03): http://libweb2.princeton.edu/rbsc2/ga/unseenhands/index.html [accessed 18 January 2020].

3   Anne Lyon Haight, "Are Women the Natural Enemies of Books?" in *Bookmaking on the Distaff Side*, New York: Distaff Side, 1937, p. 91.

4   Martha Scotford, "Toward an Expanded View of Women in Graphic Design: Messy History vs Neat History", *Visible Language* vol. 28, n. 4 (1994), pp. 368–88: http://www.marthascotford.org/wp-content/uploads/2015/12/MessyvsNeatHistory.article.pdf [accessed 27 November 2019].

Bookmaking

on the

Distaff Side

Mcmxxxvii

INTRODUCTION

Ever since the days of Mrs. Gutenberg, women have been involved in the art of printing; and now, more than ever, they are to be found in the offices and factories concerned with the making of books. Yet never before, to our knowledge, have they been organized into a group for the express purpose of producing a book by, for, and concerning themselves. *Bookmaking on the Distaff Side* is the product of their writing, their designing, their type-setting and their printing; and while it has sometimes been necessary to call in the men for the more menial tasks of the printing-office, it remains essentially a female book.

Our demurest thanks go to the various gentlemen who so kindly and so gallantly helped us, and whose names appear at the end of the various signatures. And our thanks go too to the following people and organizations whose names for one reason or another do not elsewhere appear:

Miss M. E. Stewart of J. C. Valentine & Co. for the binding.

Miss Delight Rushmore, for the binding paper.

Mr. Bennett A. Cerf, for securing the original letter from Gertrude Stein.

XXXXXXXXXXXXXXXXXXXXXX

THE ALLING & CORY COMPANY for announcements.

THE TRUART REPRODUCTION COMPANY, for the binding die.

H. P. ULICH & COMPANY, for the boxes.

ERNST REICHL of H. Wolff, for the pieces by Gertrude Stein & Louise Bonino.

THE COMMITTEE

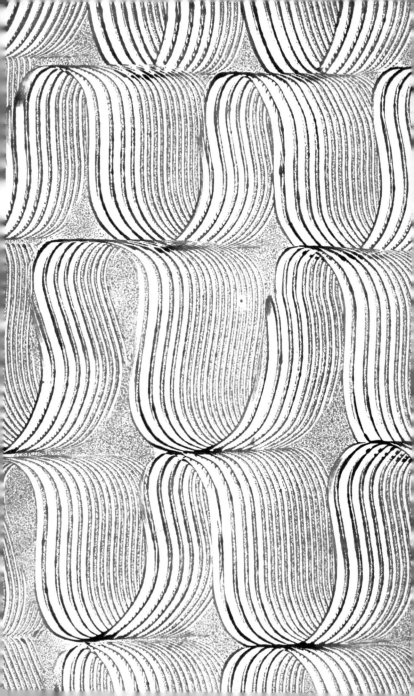

The Book as a Pot-Luck Offering: Edna Beilenson, Jane Grabhorn & the Books of the Distaff Side

Kathleen Walkup

Ever since the days of Mrs. Gutenberg, women have been involved in the art of printing; and now, more than ever, they are to be found in the offices and factories concerned with the making of books.
Yet never before, to our knowledge, have they been organized into a group for the express purpose of producing a book by, for, and concerning themselves.

In 1937, a loosely formed group of women, whose collaboration was framed around both the business and hobby of printing, produced *Bookmaking on the Distaff Side*, which was, according to their introduction, the first such book produced by and for women on the subject of women in printing. The book, an eclectic mix of articles, poems and tributes that are often humorous and occasionally apologetic, contains several well-researched essays that examine the role women have played in the history of Euro-American trade printing. Writers such as Ruth Shepard Granniss on "Printer Maids, Wives and Widows," Edna K. Rushmore on two women printers of the Colonial era in North America, and Marguerite Swanton on women who had acted as typesetters during different historical periods, pointed to the seriousness with which the women, despite a somewhat frivolous overlay, took their subject.

The group of women did not create a formal organisation. The anonymously written introduction to the book, the beginning of which is quoted above, is signed, THE COMMITTEE.

And while thanks are generously offered to various supporters of the project, the actual committee members are not listed, nor does the book offer a colophon that might have contained the names of the organisers.

The book itself was produced in an unusual and inventive manner. *Bookmaking on the Distaff Side* offers no contents page, index or list of contributors. There is a title page with no authors, editors or even publisher listed beyond the title itself, in swash italic, and the date. The dedicatory page has a bouquet designed from printer's ornaments and offered in a dingbat hand, with the words, "from BR to the Ladies." BR is the pre-eminent book designer Bruce Rogers. The position of this bouquet following the title page indicates that Rogers is the designer, not of the book, but only of the title page, although this is never noted except by the ornamental style of the page, a design motif at which Rogers was particularly adept.

This book and its sister offerings *Goudy Gaudeamus* (1939) and *The Children's Sampler* (1950) are pot-luck books. The three books were issued in bound collations of separate signatures that range from four to twenty pages, with the majority being in French-fold and thus printed on one side only. The signatures share a format for the practical purposes of binding but have no other commonality save one: the papers, typography, design and colour are different for each.

The release of these books, and in particular the first one, in this pot-luck format is never explained by the women, in 'The Committee', and explain in the preface that the book "…is the product of [women's] writing, designing, typesetting and printing, and while it has sometimes been necessary to call in the men for the more menial tasks of the printing-office, it remains essentially a female book."

The closest record of the original committee members is a small brochure, undated but almost certainly from early 1937, announcing a book that is in this brochure "tentatively entitled" *Women in Bookmaking*. The three signatories are Edna Beilenson, Evelyn Harter and Beatrice Warde. Warde's name is followed by a parenthetical notation: "(for England)". The brochure states the women's intention to publish "a sound little volume…composed of signatures contributed by Females only, about Females' past contributions, and for the advancement of the Female in these crafts." It goes on to state the book's format (4½" × 7½" trim size) and encourages entries that are "historical, factual, or fanciful" using any paper and any type, "the more diverse the style, the better!" The brochure lists the women who have already offered to contribute: Ruth Granniss (Grolier Club), Helen Gentry ("Printer"), Emily Connor (Marchbanks Press), Edna Rushmore (Golden Hind Press), Anne Heyneman ("Illustrator"), Alison Davis (Simon and Schuster) and "the three members of our Committee."

These three women had strong profiles in the 1930s New York printing and publishing arenas, in which women in general rarely figured. Beilenson was by 1937 a well-established partner in the publishing firm of Peter Pauper Press, founded by her husband Peter Beilenson before their marriage. Harter, who began her professional career as a secretary at *Scribner's Magazine* and had a stint as a teacher in a log-cabin house in rural Michigan, was a publisher and columnist in New York by the time the invitation was issued. In a late memoir, she says, "As far as I know I was the only woman in the 1930s doing a complete job of design and production for a trade house publishing 20 to 30 books a year." She left her job at Random House in 1937 to give birth to a son.[1]

The third signatory, Warde, was the only one to fail to contribute to the book. By 1937, Warde was well known in both America and in her adopted country of England as virtually the only woman writing about type and typography. Warde's earliest essays about type history were in fact written under a male pseudonym, Paul Beaujon. Beaujon's authorship of an essay about Claude Garamond, Jean Jannon and the origins of the type that would come to be called Garamond earned the author an offer in 1927 of a part-time editorship of *The Monotype Recorder*. When Warde turned up, the executives at the Monotype Corporation did

1   Evelyn Harter, "The Life or the Work", *Books at Iowa* vol. 4 (November 1984).

THE PAUL BEAUJON who has been staggering the Gelehrten, the aesthetes and the printing craftsmen hereabouts these past four weeks, is almost ready to call it a visit and return to h-- London desk. To bring h-- down to earth before h-- embarkation, *The Typophiles* wish to subject h-- to a dinner at The Amherst Club, on Monday evening, March 8*th* at 6:30.

What, you ask, *another* dinner? Well, yes; but a dinner with a difference; a dinner unmatched in downright literalness; a dinner with no headaches to anyone concerned: no ordeal by oratory, no heavy-handed declarations of formal esteem, no heavy-footed assurances of h-- supremacy in h-- chosen fields; just an *informal* family gathering where artfully spontaneous remarks will either be unmade or go unheard; in short, a simple occasion for *The Typophiles* (with some friends and *Ladies-in-Printing) to wish godspeed to an American whose activity in England partly explains the recent stimulation in the British printing trades.

PRICE IS LOW: $1.50 per person, including a draught of some British brew to be chosen by our Beverage Committee.

CAPACITY (seating, we mean) is limited to fifty. If you can be present return the card *promptly* to reserve a place. No checks or advance payment needed. The affair, remember, is *informal;* just let us know if we are to count upon your coming. There may be a surprise.

THE COMMITTEE

New York, February 26, 1937

*And don't think we haven't had a Constitutional crisis of our own!

Invitation to a dinner hosted by the Typophiles to honor Beatrice Warde, 1937.
Courtesy of Special Collections, University of Delaware Libraries.

not rescind the offer despite their surprise at her gender. In 1930, Warde gave a talk, *Printing Should be Invisible*, at the St. Bride Institute in London that would become arguably the single most quoted essay in the history of Western typography. Warde's name attached to the initial call for contributions to *Women in Bookmaking* would have helped give the project star status and authority.

It is possible that the call for contributions revolved around Warde's visit to the US from her adopted country in early 1937. On February 26th of that year an invitation was sent from the venerable New York organisation, The Typophiles. Signed by The Committee, the invitation is to a dinner honoring Warde before her return to England:

"The Paul Beaujon who has been staggering the Gelehrten [punditry], the aesthetes and the printing craftsmen hereabouts these past four weeks, is almost ready to call it a visit and return to h-- London desk." The invitation goes on to coyly refer to Warde's gender several times through the use of the censored pronoun (h--). The promise is for an informal evening devoid of the usual after-dinner speeches. The invitation refers to this as a "family gathering" of no more than 50 Typophiles "with some friends and *Ladies-in-Printing." The asterisk refers to a footnote, "*And don't think we haven't had a Constitutional crisis of our own!" While again there is no explanation of the crisis the "Ladies" may be experiencing, the suggestion is that a type of gendered revolt in the spirit of

Edward VIII's professed love for the American divorcée may be in the offing. The fact that Warde is referred to by her male pseudonym only emphasises this issue.

The driving force behind the project was undoubtedly Beilenson. Through her work at Peter Pauper Press, she established a reputation as a graphic designer that was nearly unique in the completely male dominated field of American design during the 1930s, 1940s and 1950s. In 1949, Harvard University published a compilation of essays on book design, *Graphic Forms: The Arts as Related to the Book*, in which Beilenson was the sole woman among heralded designers and artists such as Paul Rand, W.A. Dwiggins and György Kepes. Her essay, "Experimentation", while mentioning only male designers, denies the existence of separate areas of "feminine" and "masculine" design.

Beilenson appreciated colour in her design work, and often saturated the Peter Pauper publications with vibrant and folk art-inspired lettering and images. One hallmark of Beilenson's editorial approach was small format gift books, including a series called *The ABCs of Cookery* that in turn prompted several cookery titles such as *Holiday Party Desserts*. The most notorious of the cookery books was *Cooking to Kill: The Poison Cookbook*. Credited to one Ebenezer Murgatroyd, the book was unquestionably written in Beilenson's wryly humorous voice. The accompanying "comic drawings" were done by an actual illustrator, Herb Roth.

Title pages, *Holiday Party Desserts*, Peter Pauper Press, 1951, and (overleaf) *Cooking to Kill: The Poison Cookbook*, Peter Pauper Press, 1956, written and designed by Edna Beilenson. Courtesy of the author.

"GEE WILLIKERS, UNCLE OSBERT, YOU
MEAN TO SAY YOU *LIKE* IT?"

COOKING TO KILL!

The Poison Cook-book

Comic Recipes for the Ghoul, Cannibal, Witch & Murderer. Stewing and potting mothers-in-law. Tested recipes for spoiled brats, business rivals, and strayed lovers. Cannibal picnic meat. Sure-fire salads. How to make your friends die laughing!

RECIPES BY EBENEZER MURGATROYD
COMIC DRAWINGS BY HERB ROTH

Peter Pauper Press, Mount Vernon, N.Y.

Oh

please be my valentine
I'll be good I'll be
fine
I'll be quick I'll be
clever
I wont ever leave you
ever
ii
You may think that
I'm too passionate
but this is strong
I just cant ration it‑
iii
and this has been an
awful winter
oh god! it's hard to be
a printer.

'Oh please be my valentine,' Jane Grabhorn, author and printer.
In *The Compleat Jane Grabhorn*, Arion Press, 1968. Courtesy of the author.

The inclusion of several comic entries in *Bookmaking on the Distaff Side* attests to a shared affinity with humor by the book's contributors. Essays like Madeline Forgue's "Beaten to a Pulp", written from the point of view of a bathtub turned paper vat, lighten the tone, none more so than Grabhorn's "A Typographic Discourse for the Distaff Side of Printing, a book by ladies." Grabhorn was the wife of one of the famous San Francisco Grabhorn brothers, whose Grabhorn Press was central to the development of that city in becoming an American centre of fine press printing and publishing. And while Grabhorn contributed a good deal of work to the Grabhorn Press, from bookkeeping to typesetting to hand binding, her irrepressible nature found a home in her own imprint, Jumbo Press. Grabhorn named her operation after a table-top printing press that she purchased for her own use, away from the commercial production of her husband and his brother. On it she printed her own pronouncements about printing, all of which poked fun at the traditional and staid world of fine press work. In "A Typographic Discourse," Grabhorn demonstrates, in nonsensical verse, her disdain for conventional word breaks and the tyranny of precise spacing when setting text in metal type:

> "At this kind of trif-eling, let the male wallow, for women the freedom of wind and of swallow."

Grabhorn also formed a partnership with William Matson Roth and, briefly, Jane Swinerton, to publish an eclectic list of trade books under the Colt Press imprint. Her publications for Colt Press included her own collection of cookbooks (although nothing in the vein of *Cooking to Kill*) as well as fiction by important writers such as fellow California dwellers Janet Lewis and Frank Norris. But it was Grabhorn's work under the Jumbo Press imprint that gave her joy and a release from the exacting work at Grabhorn Press. "Jumbo became Jane's escape, her vehicle for self-expression during the rest of her life, as she sought personal recognition rather than being in the shadow of the brothers Grabhorn... She once wrote, 'Now Fine Printing is supposed to be so difficult that only Gutenberg and the Grabhorns ever really did it. But Jumbo has long scoffed at this myth. Jumbo Press says Printing is as easy as the Printer wants it to be.'"

Given the sometimes raucous and irreverent contributions to *Bookmaking on the Distaff Side* (in addition to Grabhorn's and Forgue's pieces, there is Harter's "An Interview With The Eminent Professor Hugo. K.O. Muttonquad", Anne Lyon Haight's "Are Women the Natural Enemies of Books?", Barbara Cowles' and Ellen Bentley's "The Printer's Mistress to His Wife", and Mary D. Alexander's "A Few Disadvantages of Being a Woman"), Beilenson's own contribution is somewhat puzzling. Titled "Men in Printing", the short piece lists eleven men well known in the fine printing trade, including her own husband. While the brief listings are written with her tongue firmly in her cheek (the paragraph on her husband dwells entirely on the domestic and mentions his habit of snatching the sheet off the bed), these tributes to Frederic Goudy, Bruce Rogers and the rest read like an apologia to the men who may take umbrage at the nature of the book these women have put together.

Whether or not the gender revolt was being back-pedalled by Beilenson in her essay, the issue of gender defensiveness seems clear in the ultimate choice of title. In early 1937, the book was referred to in the initial call for contributions as *Women in Bookmaking*. That title appears twice, once at the head of the brochure and again, in small capitals, in the body. The return form, which takes up the last of the four pages of the brochure, states, "This is the best idea since the Suffragette Movement." The return form suggests several possible topics that contributors might consider: Women Collectors, Women Binders, Women Engravers, Printing Widows, Woman's Place in the Private Press Movement. Only two, "On the Art of Being a Printer's Wife", and "What Mrs. Estienne Said When Robert Installed His New Hand Press", suggest a comic take on the subject matter.

By the time of its release late in the year, the comic contributions number at least seven of the 31 entries, and the title had become *Bookmaking on the Distaff Side*. While the term

RETURN FORM

This is the best idea since the Suffragette Movement, and you may certainly count on me for . . . printing; . . . literary matter; . . . art work; . . . sundry.

My subject matter will be . . . .

August First is the Deadline

Suggestions

Women Collectors   Women Engravers
Women Binders   Printing Widows
Woman's Place in the Private Press Movement
On the Art of Being a Printer's Wife
What Mrs. Estienne Said When Robert Installed His
    New Hand Press

Count on me for the dinner . . . . . .

Name   . . . .
Address . . . .
            . . . .

Return to Edna Beilenson, 629 MacQuesten Parkway North, Mount Vernon, New York, at your earliest convenience.

Request for contributions to a book about women and printing sent by 'The Committee', 1937. Courtesy of Special Collections, University of Delaware Libraries.

"distaff" would have carried fewer anti-feminist overtones in the 1930s, its use had decreased significantly since 1800. Distaff is a word defined by its counterpart, staff. In genealogy, the staff or spear represents the male side of the family, the distaff its female counterpart. Thus the distaff side is the female side but defined in the negative, that is, the non-male. The term was further applied to a tool for spinning, which was women's work. Changing the title from the active form—*Women in Bookmaking*—to its passive cousin—*Bookmaking on the Distaff Side*—significantly shifts the intention of the work from a pro-active work by women that celebrates their contributions to the field, to a more passive treatise offered in apologetic counterpoint to the male field.

In the "Author's Introduction" to a chapbook in memory of his wife Bertha, the type designer and printer Frederic Goudy (who contributed an essay about Bertha to *Bookmaking on the Distaff Side*) confirms this more timid take on the book:

"In the spring of 1937, certain young women 'involved in the art of printing' decided to follow in the steps of The Typophiles and produce a book—a book about women in printing—largely by themselves in the writing, and also in its actual manufacture." Goudy then goes on to explain that he was invited to contribute a piece about Bertha (who died in 1935) by Beilenson, whom Goudy describes only as the "wife of one of our younger distinguished book makers", despite Beilenson's central role at Peter Pauper Press. Goudy does go on to sing

Beilenson's praises in the highest terms, stating that her "great ability made her known, by name, at least, to more people interested in typography than any other woman in America."[2]

The Typophiles was a likely candidate for both sparking the inspiration for *Bookmaking on the Distaff Side* and creating some barriers to the book. An organisation formed in New York in the early 1930s, The Typophiles was a male-only group, an exclusion that lasted until 1970. The men met monthly at various restaurants to swap stories, jokes and, inevitably in these settings, jobs. That women were excluded from the meetings meant not only that they were spared some of the sexist discussion that would have taken place; it also would have kept women from hearing about job openings or, should any of them want to be employed as printers, the work that they might have otherwise been available to do.

There was one exception to the male-only rule. Because her reputation was cemented under the pseudonym Paul Beaujon, the argument went, Warde was awarded a place at The Typophiles table. It is as likely that Warde's connection with Stanley Morison and Eric Gill, as well as the fact that she posed nude for some of Gill's woodcuts, played a part in her invitation to join The Typophiles. (And since she lived in England, she was not likely to attend many meetings.) While Warde may or may

2   Frederic Goudy, *Bertha M. Goudy: Recollections by one who knew her best*, New York: Village Press, 1939, p. 3.

not have relished being one of the boys, her signal presence in The Typophiles provided a powerful incentive for her role as one of "The Committee" initiating a book about women in the bookmaking fields. That Warde gave her support to the project at its initial stage indicates both that she believed in the mission and that she must have recognised her unique place in helping the book move forward.

Of course, The Typophiles' approach to creating a small series of books by soliciting signatures in specific sizes that were then bound together undoubtedly inspired The Committee to initiate their pot-luck book about women and printing. The first such Typophiles book was in fact a *Festschrift* to honor none other than Frederic Goudy on his 70th birthday in 1935. The Typophiles would go on to create six more projects in this manner. For The Committee, this pot-luck approach would make an otherwise nearly impossible project—to record the contributions of women in the printing and related trades—manageable.

If women couldn't join The Typophiles (or for that matter nearly any of the other professional and collectors' clubs proliferating across the US), they could form their own organisations, and did. One such group was the Club of Printing Women (CPW), founded in New York in 1930 as a forum for "the interchange of ideas and experience". The idea for the Club, as it was known, grew out of a meeting of the Printing Estimators Club of New York, which devoted its May 1930 meeting to the topic of

"Women in Printing". Three women spoke at that meeting, all in executive or ownership positions in the printing trade. Two of them, Dorothy Doty and Annie L. Green, joined three colleagues in identifying a list of 31 women who held executive positions in the printing industry in New York. When 22 of these women met for dinner to discuss forming an organisation, they listed their work as secretaries but also as estimators, sales women, art directors, owners and presidents. Their first organisational protocols centred on the criteria for membership. Writing 25 years later on the genesis of the Club, Biruta Sesnan recalls the questions being, "What would be the qualifications for membership? Would the Club be confined to executives only? How would an executive be defined? What about women in the allied trades?"

The debate was initially settled by requiring that any woman joining the Club be affiliated with the New York Employing Printers Association, a trade organisation that provided support but came with unspecified obligations, according to Sesnan. The affiliation, which ended during the Depression, didn't help to expand the membership in the Club, which remained at 30 through World War Two. The issue of allied trade affiliation (binding, papermaking and other related trades that employed women) was solved by a quota system that stipulated membership of at least 60% printing and no more than 40% allied trades. The main activity of the club involved visits to "places of printing interest" such as the production plant of the *New York Times* and a linotype assembly plant in Brooklyn.

The Club struggled with the issue of inclusion of women involved in the printing trades, as opposed to those in administrative positions, and even whether a woman involved in the fledgling offset trade was actually "in printing", but the group remained one culled from the executive ranks. In 1937, the Club did its part to support the idea that "now more than ever" women were involved with printing by contributing a signature, albeit a quite modest one of four pages, to *Bookmaking on the Distaff Side*. In their contribution Sesnan says that "The printing industry finds women at the case and the typesetting machine, in the proof room and the bindery . . . .", but on the next page she states that the organisation has remained "essentially informal".

Beilenson was never a member of CPW, nor was Harter, the second of the three "Committee" members. If Warde, the third Committee member, was given honorary membership in CPW, there is no record of it. In fact, only two of the contributors to *Bookmaking on the Distaff Side*, Priscilla Crane (who wrote an introduction to the poems of Anne Bradstreet) and Lucina Wakefield (who contributed a hand-coloured woodcut to an unattributed poem), are listed as having been members of CPW between 1930 and 1955. And only one, Emily Connor of Marchbanks Press, appears on the roster of CPW members for its 25th anniversary publication about its history,

Antique, Modern & Swash. Connor, who was also a past president (1932–33) of CPW, is one of the six women included in Green's essay, "A Few First Ladies in Printing in New York in the Twentieth Century".

The reasons why there is so little commonality between the two organisations (one claiming informality while having officers and regular meetings, the other having no formal structure) are not recorded. One reason would no doubt be geography; the full name of the CPW was the Club of Printing Women of New York, and some of the women simply lived elsewhere. With no club quarters, there would have been no incentive for women to join from a distance. Given the ongoing challenge within CPW to firmly identify its core constituency other than by gender, some women may have had difficulty seeing themselves in the organisation. Women whose primary work was as part of their husband's enterprises, for instance, could have decided not to align themselves with the professional women in the organisation. Marie Carré Phelps, whose essay "Bookbinding in the Home" talks about filling her "leisure hours" as a primarily self-taught binder, most likely did not see herself as a member of a professional organisation. (Despite her modest self-presentation, she nonetheless mentions that her interest in binding led her to interests in "papermaking, printing, illustration, illuminating and woodcuts", all of which she researched as part of her work.) Granniss, who contributed a compendious but well-researched essay on the history of women and printing ("Printer Maids, Wives and Widows"), was librarian at the Grolier Club and therefore too much into the ancillary category for CPW membership.

Beilenson, whose home and business were located in Mount Vernon, a New York City suburb, was hardly out of geographical range. She joined Peter Pauper the same year that CPW was founded, in 1930, and may not have seen herself as part of a professional organisation at that point in her young career (she was 21 when she married Peter and joined the press).

But the lack of crossover between CPW and The Distaff Side is intriguing. The very modest contribution of CPW to *Bookmaking on the Distaff Side* (four pages, as mentioned, containing four paragraphs of simple black type, along with a typographic title that says simply "CPW") could suggest that the two organisations had different outlooks and goals. On the other hand, the simplicity of the CPW contribution could be a reflection of the members' focus on administrative aspects of printing rather than graphic ones.

CPW also contributed, again modestly, to the next publication by The Distaff Side. *Goudy Gaudeamus*, issued in 195 copies in 1939, was a celebration of the beloved type designer and printer Frederic Goudy after a fire destroyed his Village Press. (The fire was the second to completely decimate the press. The first took place when Beilenson was still alive.)

Goudy Gaudeamus is another pot-luck book. This time four women signed the introduction: Beilenson and Harter are joined by Connor and Fanny Duschnes who was, with her husband Philip, a New York rare bookseller. The introduction explains why contributions are not limited to those of "the ladies"; people of "all genders" want to celebrate the famous and beloved Goudy. In addition to CPW, The Typophiles, the American Institute for Graphic Arts and Advertising Agencies' Service Company, Inc., all have contributions that intersect with those from some of the women (Grabhorn, Wakefield, three of the four Committee members and some others) who contributed to the original volume. The book even contains a reproduction of a short letter of condolence about the fire along with birthday wishes from First Lady Eleanor Roosevelt.

The book's turnaround time was highly impressive. Conceived after the mid-January fire, it was presented at The Distaff Side Dinner in Goudy's honor on his 74th birthday, 8 March 1939. The elaborate menu (Supreme of Fruit Florida, Boned Stuffed Squab Chicken Polonaise and Mocha Rum Cake, among other delicacies) and dancing were overseen by Mistress of Ceremonies Beilenson, who received all-cap headline billing on the printed programme, with the other three members of The Distaff Side Committee sharing further responsibilities. Beilenson's name, along with most of the rest of the programme, was set in Truesdell Italic, a typeface designed by Goudy in 1930. The drawings and matrices were completely lost in the 1939 fire.

Although the publishing activity of The Distaff Side was curtailed during World War Two, the women "sponsored a mammoth Carnival of Books", after which a "substantial check" was sent to Bundles for Britain.[3] In 1950, The Distaff Side published its third and final pot-luck book, *A Children's Sampler.* Subtitled *Selections from famous children's books, printed with care and solicitude by the ladies of The Distaff Side, in the year of our Lord 1950*, the book contains 14 sections of excerpts ranging from original work by Haight ("Morals, Manners, Etiquette and the Three R's from the Sixth to the Sixteenth Century") to sample pages of an imaginary book by the renowned designer W.A. Dwiggins to "Five Chinese Fairy Tales". While Haight and Grabhorn, two women who contributed to the first two Distaff Side volumes, do so again here, many of the names are new. The Introduction is signed only by "Edna Beilenson for The Distaff Side." And while she claims that the "unselfish character" of the women of The Distaff Side have given "unsparingly of their time, money and energies in a spirit of cooperation which has seen each project to completion", the lack of signatories to the Introduction, the edition size (375 copies) and the generally much slicker and more polished look of *A Children's Sampler* suggests that the central energy for the project stemmed from Beilenson herself, with help from

3   Edna Beilenson, "The Distaff Side: By way of introduction", *A Children's Sampler*, no publisher, no place, 1950.

some well-connected friends in graphic design and printing. All proceeds went to children with cardiac health problems.

A scattering of other titles appeared from time to time that claimed a connection with The Distaff Side, but in essence their legacy consists primarily of their first book, along with the two additional titles. Beilenson would go on to become the first woman to preside over the American Institute of Graphic Arts, among other honors. After her husband's death in 1962, she continued publishing under the Peter Pauper Press imprint until her death in 1981.

A Typografic Discourse ✦

for The Distaff Side of Printing, a book by ladies

From Jane Grabhorn's typographic laboratory
Jumbo Press San Francisco 1937

The mighty elephant

is now

Under Way

FOREWORD:

Mad, abandoned, the Jumbo Press is revolutionizing the printing world turn ing it upside down and topsy turvy, exp osing all its hoodoo voodoo, and divest ing its weird ceremonies of all their gla mour. Jumbo stripped the mask from ty pography's Medicine Men and their di sciples have seen them as they are: pom pous tottering pretenders, mouthing con ceits and sweating decadence.

Three typographic tenets

developed in the Elephant's laboratory

The tenets are 3 (see A Guide and H andbook for Amateurs of Printing):

1 ⁃ Do not hyphenate your words. This i s not because the effect thus achieved is novel and thereby striking in appearanc e, but because of the beautiful logic of s uch procedure. Consider these things, la dies, and allow those qualities so peculi ar to the female⁃ courage, imaginativene ss, adaptability, & the will to experimen t⁃ oh give them their head and let the res ults be caustic, spangled pages of type sh ot thru the heavens of paper and ink.

☞ Do not like mimicking mem ory⁃doped moppets chanting 'i before e except after c' waste precious hours sy

llablizing and wrinkling your pretty lit
tle brows. Now that the first shock is ov
er do you not read this with normal ease
? (allright allright, but Gutenberg hims
elf could not have gotten that question
mark on the end of that line). A summ
ary of this important tenet now follows i
n simple jingle form for the youngsters:

Either rape your words with
out shame or abash--
For a hyphen is at best an emasculat
ed dash--
Or a lionhearted printer you had bet
ter be
And let the letters fall according to
their destiny.

END OF TENET NUMBER ONE

technique and the fallacy of its overemp
hasis. It is allright to know the names of
the types & to be able to recognize them
at a glance; and it may be a great satisfac
tion to know the mathematics and theor
y of type sizes. But it is folly to waste mu
ch time on all this. What goes with Gar
amond? Anything and everything. Bod
oni? Well that's different; Bodoni goes
out the window. But a fine page should
have on it, for instance, Goudy black let
ter, Italian Oldstyle italic, Garamond la
rge caps, and a Centaur ampersand; the
n in rapid succession, Caslon Janson D
eepdene Poliphilus Lutetia⸌ and so on
until the page is full. Printers sound like

this as they meditate over the 'design' of a title page (always a title page; very few printers bother to meditate over a text p age):

" How does this look? "

" Superb, Jo, superb. Too bad those types don't go together so we could use it."

Jumbo herself suffers from the condesce nsion of her mate ⁄a lordly fellow⁄ who a long time ago mastered the works & b iographies of all the printers since the be ginning of printing. He can also spot th e name of a type and spit on the dot of it s eye ten yards away. Also this marvelou s male periodically corners Jumbo and r attles off a terrifying group of figures evid ently designed to demonstrate with what ease a person, providing he has inside in formation, can use certain sizes of spaces with different size type and they will fit. Something like that. For Jumbo's part, she roots around until she finds somethi ng she wants. And with what a glad & mighty trumpet call is it welcomed! Th e rafters tremble with the sound of the lit tle elephant's joy.

𝕯on't be tied down like dunces and fools
𝕿o quads ems picas and man made rules.
𝕴n this kind of trif-eling, let the male wallow,
𝕱or women the freedom of wind and of swallow.

END OF TENET NUMBER TWO ^{give thanks & take a deep breath} ✤

give thanks & take
a deep breath ✤

is about corrections and people who make them

About corrections Jumbo feels very stro ngly as follows: do not make them. The greatest thrill the Reader has is margin marking. He rips through a book espec ially if he is a printer, crossing out an 'o' here, putting in a 't' there, even in plac es jotting THIS IS NOT TRUE!!!!! with a flourish. If he is not a printer, he will make broad assertions about typog raphy too. If he is a printer, he will say there is not enough ink or there is too m uch. If he has the true spirit of the colle ctor (predominantly a male affliction), he will sit down and write a long letter t o the printer smugly noting all errors, & ending wistfully, 'These are only a few of the more serious mistakes; time does not permit the listing of them all.' He means he hasn't found any more of cou rse, but leave him be. It is a rather quai nt pastime for people these days. The id ea that anything so harmless could amu se a fairly large group of humans in this age of sinister pleasures should be enco uraged.

The kindly printer lets things be-
Hark to some Jumbo philosophy:

From other elephants this one differs
This elephant always forgets
The mistakes she makes and the shocking spacing
On every page she sets.

The Vampire and

the Darling Priest

of Modernism

Ida Börjel

"As I say a motor car goes on, but my
business my ultimate business as an artist
was not with where the car goes as it goes
but with the movement inside that is
the essence of its going."
Gertrude Stein, *Portraits and Repetition*
(1935)

"Agreed: an ill-matched correspondence
Entwines us each with each, and all with all."
Laura Riding, *A Letter to Any Friend* (1935)

In 1929, Gertrude Stein's lecture *An
Acquaintance With Description* was published
by poet, prose writer, essayist, critic (and later
language theorist) Laura Riding and poet
Robert Graves. The two of them had owned and
managed Seizin Press for two years by the time.
At the centre, or at least in the middle, of their
apartment in St Peter's Square in London, stood
a Crown Albion hand press from 1872, fitted
with a Caslon font. It wasn't the most recent
model, but it worked well enough.

The Albion was reliable, even though
it wasn't particularly light. Still, it was lighter
and less bulky than other hand presses, the
Stanhope for example. Albion was known to
be powerful, even very much so, especially
when it came to smaller printed matter. Albion
would become the most popular hand press in
the UK, similar to the Washington model in the
US. Albion had a slightly different toggle lever.
As a whole, it was more compact, but, for the
amateur, not so easy to manoeuvre.

Patience, patience. Their friend Vyvyan Richards became a fixture in the Riding-Graves home for a number of months; she became their mentor, teaching them printing, and providing advice. Since she had a printing press herself she was knowledgeable.

Riding and Graves had used an advance on one of Graves' books to pay for their Albion. They'd probably had enough of publishers meddling in the work, enough of misprints and commercialism. The desire for counteraction was evident already in the couple's *A Survey of Modernist Poetry* (1927) and *A Pamphlet Aginst Anthologies* (1928), where they introduced a new method of close reading, which would become crucial for the New Criticism school of American literary theory. Perhaps Riding had also, as she writes in the preface to *The Progress of Stories* (1935), grown tired of accusations that she was obscure, of being made scapegoat "for the incapacity of people to understand what they only pretend to want to know."

At the time, as Jerome J. McGann writes in his 1993 study of Modernism *Black Riders*, something close to a movement of small publishers who, in possession of their own printing presses, opposed the commercial book production of bigger publishers, was budding. Most bigger publishers didn't look beyond novels; contemporary readers wanted more pages for less money.

Seizin. The word is an archaic term for *possession, ownership*. To take over the means of production, and by doing so also take control over the conditions *for* production. To seek space for freer thought—to create the conditions that liberate the shape of the thought from the shape of the book page, or the demands of a bookseller. With an independently owned press, Riding's genre-bending, page breaks, and notions about design were demands accommodated from within the creative process, in the sense that the idea no longer had to contort itself to standard formatting.

A new way of doing things, but with old methods? In purely financial terms, the results were mediocre, even pretty bad. Considering the price, what costs could be accepted? At any rate, Riding wanted to publish "necessary books by particular people", "decidedly not addressed to the collector but to those interested in work rather than printing." First, she published one of her own: Seizin One was *Love as Love, Death as Death* (1928), at 64 pages and in an edition of 175 (not a negligible number at the time).

Seizin Two became Gertrude Stein's *An Acquaintance with Description*, in 1929. Two years earlier, Riding published an essay in the avant-garde journal *transition*, titled "Gertrude Stein and the New Barbarism", in which she, with some noticeable ambivalence, writes about Stein that she "is perhaps the only artisan of language who has ever succeeded in practicing scientific barbarism literally. Her words are primitive in the sense that they are bare, immobile, mathematically placed, abstract." Stein was the only one who dared to be simple, primitive, dumb, and barbaric enough to succeed in barbarism, Riding wrote, adding that Stein was "the darling priest of modernism [...] if her age but knew it."

The bards of history, in this case the respective official biographers of Riding and Graves, provide divergent accounts of how Stein's manuscript came into being. According to Richard Perceval Graves, Riding and Graves travelled abroad to meet with Stein in the summer of 1928, and Stein, taken by Riding's sexual magnetism, immediately wrote a book for the couple. Elizabeth Friedmann, however, writes in *A Mannered Grace: The Life of Laura Riding Jackson*, that Riding and Stein had been corresponding after Riding's criticism of Stein's work, and this created a desire in both of them to meet. When they finally got together in Paris in the summer of 1928, they had already agreed to publish *An Acquaintance With Description* with Seizin.

In Stein's *Autobiography of Alice B. Toklas* (1933), another story emerges: "It was during this summer that Gertrude Stein began two long things...It led first to *An Acquaintance With Description*, afterwards printed by the Seizin Press. She began at this time to describe landscape as if anything she saw was a natural phenomenon, a thing existent in itself, and she found it, this exercise, very interesting and it finally led her to the later series of Operas and Plays. I am trying to be as commonplace as I can be, she used to say to me. And then sometimes a little worried, it is not too commonplace."

Half a year later, in early 1929, Riding saw her ménage à trois disintegrate. In desperation, she drank Lysol in front of Graves, his wife, and the Irish poet Geoff Gibbs, and then jumped out of a fourth-floor window. It is reported that Graves jumped after her, from the third floor. Both of them survived; the police called her a "vampire". Riding broke her pelvis and fractured her spine. It was said she would never be able to walk again, but she miraculously recuperated. High on morphine in her sick bed, she reportedly asked for Stein, who shortly sent her reply in a letter to Graves: "Laura is so poignant and so upright and she gets into your tenderness as well as your interest and I am altogether heartbroken about her, I cannot come now. But tell her and keep telling her that we want her with us. I had an unhappy feeling that Laura would have sooner or later a great disillusionment and it would have to come through a certain vulgarity in another and it will make Laura a very wonderful person, in a strange way, a destruction and recreation of her purification but all this does not help pain and I am very closely fond of you all. Tell her all and everything from me and tell her above all that she will come to us and reasonably soon and all my love."

Riding described the situation in one of the first poems of her convalescence:

> What to say when the spider
> Say when the spider what
> The spider does what

Does does dies does it not
Not live and then not
Legs legs then none

Right before, or not long thereafter, Riding printed *An Acquaintance With Description*. Stein signed little notes, which were returned to London to be inserted into the books. The book was 50 pages long and published in a limited edition of 225. The cover was structured bone white, 21 × 14.5 cm, and on the spine, the letters shone in gold.

Following the scandalous suicide attempt, Riding and Graves escaped London's coteries, taking their love and their printing press in all its heft—800 kg—to a small house in Deià, Mallorca. Consumables were mailed at regular intervals from England. Riding began to plan a broader catalogue, including both more complex and more commercial titles. Seizin entered an alliance with London publisher Constable, a collaboration that would last until 1937. It included the magazine *Epilogue*, which, thanks to Riding as editor for the unusual composition of literary, social, and cultural criticism, came to have a great influence on the literary circles in the pre-World War Two period.

What were the routines like at the press? In a response to a letter from a friend, Riding replied, "How's that? How's anything you know or don't? […] on ordinary paper […] Printed by myself, and Robert […] Yes, I ink, he pulls, we patch a greyness […] Or clean the thickened letters out […]."

Was it financially viable? *An Acquaintance With Description* retailed for 11 shilling and 6 pence at the bookseller William Bain in London. In the 1920s, a new novel normally cost around 8 shilling and 6 pence, which was a fifth of an industrial worker's weekly salary. Non-fiction was even more expensive. The pricing of Seizin's books essentially put them out of reach of the working class. Political radicals were presumably not among those Riding wanted to reach. The concept, as she described it, was an audience of readers and writers with a special interest.

Stein's *An Acquaintance With Description* can be interpreted as an idiosyncratic comment on her once-teacher William James' ontological discussion in his great work *The Principles of Psychology*, and on Bertrand Russell's *Knowledge by Acquaintance and Knowledge by Description*, which both probe the question of what we can claim to know when we have knowledge of something through description, versus what we can claim to know through direct acquaintance. Through praxis, Stein shows that sentences can have meaning without referring to anything we know as truth. A proposition can be deemed false without it being nonsensical. Her exploration is empirical, practical, and focused on the perception of concrete reality —staying away from allegory, metaphor, and complex word choices.

Perhaps it was the notion that modernism demanded a new kind of telling that brought Riding and Stein together. Their connection began and ended with letter writing. Charismatic, independent, razor-sharp, initiated, intractable in their artistry and perhaps in their views of themselves—somewhat surprisingly, there is little research on their influences and collaboration.

Their letters are full of conversations about letter writing. This was an era where epistolary collections like the very popular *Everybody's Letter-Writer* taught the art of letter writing—and people did indeed write massive amounts of letters. Riding's little book *Four Unposted Letters to Catherine* (Hours Press, Paris, 1930, edition of 200) was full of life advice to Graves' then eight-year-old daughter like "People are for themselves when they're themself". The second edition was dedicated to Stein, with the words: "Dear Gertrude./The function of Opinion is to be that which does not get posted. Hating Opinion and loving All That Gets Posted as you do, you must applaud my not posting these letters, however much you deplore my writing them./Love,/Laura." She was assuming that Stein would dislike the publication of some-thing that should have stayed within the private sphere, and so chooses confrontation—by publishing it.

In another letter to Stein, Riding writes as though there were no contention, requesting a contribution to what would become the epistolary collection and study *Everybody's Letters* (1933): "I'm making a Compendium of All True Letters […] If you come across any good ones that won't need too much editing and the writers have gone away […] there must be thousands of true letters both to and from yearning for recognition in Paris."

Everybody's Letters is a collection of contemporary letters from friends and acquaintances (with their names changed). Several of these letter writers are unknown, for example the young Norwegian widow who writes her life's story to a British novelist after having only seen one of his books. "I send you this as the best I have to give away and you may do with it as you please." Riding categorises her letter under "universal letters", defined as those which the writer pens to tell herself stories, "as if it were all the personified fascination of all the imaginable listeners". In a universal letter, Riding notes, the letter writer's relationship to the addressee has often not begun or has already ended, and what happens to the letter, if it does get sent, is of less importance. Another question of interest to Riding was how literature is distinguished from letter writing when nearly all people can write letters. Her answer: where a letter can be "humanly and hatefully intelligent", poetry does something else, and can be "humanly stupid and artless". Moreover, she contends, letters are written to release emotional tension, whereas poems more often come into being to formulate an intellectual intensity. Riding further writes, "You must agree with me that the relation between letter writers is unfriendly, though the magic essence of letters consists in a friendly concealment of the fact."

Riding's Everybody's Letters and Stein's Everybody's Autobiography, published in 1937 (as a follow-up to the success of *Autobiography of Alice B. Toklas*). A coincidence that looks intentional. How come they sought each other out, where did their letter writing take them, and why did they turn away from each other? According to one version, Riding lost patience over Stein's last letters, which were just page upon page about her dog, the poodle Basket, and its manner of lapping water. Henceforth, and until the end of her life, Riding would write about Stein's work and personality with harsh criticism. According to another version, it was Stein who stopped answering Riding's letters, and the description of the dog lapping was in fact a key to her continued poetics and the distinction between sentences and paragraphs.

In 1933, Riding wrotes to her friend and colleague Jacob Bronowski that Seizin would cease publishing. "It is altogether too expensive and time-taking a business for us here ..." Roderick Cave notes in *Private Presses*, a book about the small presses of this period, that the commercial viability and the increased demand for popular titles meant that small imprints became dependent on larger publishers and their printing abilities, which most often led to the demise of smaller publishers.

Riding and Graves left their home on Mallorca on August 2, 1936, a few weeks after the start of the Spanish Civil War. They could only bring one suitcase on board the war ship. The old printing press was left behind. The last book marked Seizin / Constable was Riding's own *A Trojan Ending* (1937).

A decade later, Riding publicly distanced herself from poetry, on the grounds that it was not compatible with the truth. Instead, she threw herself into the management of a citrus farm in Florida, which she, now named Laura (Riding) Jackson, ran together with Schuyler B. Jackson in order to finance their life's work, an unorthodox thesaurus intended to distil every word to a single inherent and true definition. *Rational Meaning: A New Foundation for the Definition of Words* was published posthumously by University Press of Virginia, in 1997.

Nevertheless, Riding did publish a book again in 1967: her truth manifesto, *The Telling*, in which she argues for a different type of necessary telling: "We can best defend ourselves against those who would crowd us all into a prison of shrunken-destiny ... by knowing our missing story, and dwelling in it, as in the home of our thought. Let them move us to take our souls fully unto ourselves, and to speak from soul-self to one another as ourselves in truth: that speaking will be our story, and it will silence them. To defeat them we need only to tell our truth, which is theirs also." "Our truth," she continues, "cannot be all-told, from the beginning told, unless we tell it to one another."

Stein, on the other hand, continued her own quest for truth after her exchange with Riding, through the exploration and representation of description. As she had already noted in her immense *The Making of Americans* (1925): "I was realising beginning realising that everything described would not do any more than tell all

I knew about anything why should I tell all I knew about anything since after all I did not know all I knew about everything."

It does not appear that she was particularly preoccupied with Riding and their interpersonal sympathies and aversions. Stein at last found her long-desired success with *Autobiography of Alice B. Toklas*, first published in New York in 1933 by Harcourt, Brace & Co. I have not been able to trace what printing press was used. But the original edition of the book can be found online, with descriptions like: "Book Condition: Good. First Edition. Stated First Edition. Binding is bent or rolled. Spine cloth has darkened. Corners are bumped. Previous owner's name in ink on the front end paper. Small blue pencil note on the front ned board. Binding is tight and the pages are clean."

Nevertheless, Stein did, in her way, provide a glimpse of her friend / enemy/colleague / competitor in *How to Write* (1931): "An adjective have to be faced. An adjective in sound based on fugitives. Leave roads alone. They will be pleased. To cover it with whoever it is only there. An adjective they will have had May. May Rider. Mary Riding. Minna Riding, Martha Riding, Melanchta Riding. Thank you."

The Crown Albion Press on which Robert Graves and Laura Riding printed several of their works under the Seizin Press imprint at Graves' and Riding's house in Deià (Mallorca, Spain). Creative Commons Attribution-Share Alike 4.0 International. Photograph: Manuel Ramírez Sánchez.

I remember and this was long ago they were talking about automobiles and they were saying what one was and what another was and a man there who had had them from the beginning said well all I can say about automobiles perhaps some are better than others but all automobiles are good. That is the way I feel about printing, as long as printing prints words I like them when they print my words I like it best naturally enough but all words have to be printed and I like it when it is printing. To be sure I do have feelings about margins I do not like big ones, I like little ones, you might say that that is natural as I like words to be printed and when the margins are big you have less of them, I must say I liked enormously the printing of Geographical History of America, it's about the best printing I have ever seen of a purely commercial book, but even aside from with big margins there being less words than with little ones I like the way it looks best with very small ones, I have even dreamed that there might be none, but then it would not be a book, and then I made Maurice Derantiere print one with almost none, and it was a book. Let me see what else about printing when I was very young my brother and I had a printing press a very little one but we never did get to do any more than print visiting cards I do not think we ever printed any words that were not names and never since then have I done any printing. American books look very different from English and certainly from french ones, I wonder which I like best, naturally American ones. Gertrude Stein

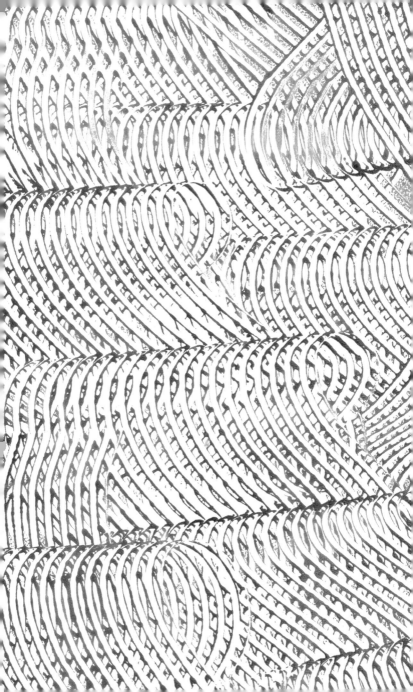

A Darn Good Idea[1]:

Feminist Printers and

the Women's Liberation

Movement in Britain

Jess Baines

1   "A darn good idea" was how Angela Cooper from
Amazon Press described the collective feeling about instigating
a women's printshop in Manchester in the mid-1970s, in an
interview with the author, 2013.

Print culture was central to the Women's Liberation Movement (WLM) that burgeoned in 1970s Britain, with a gamut of flyers and newsletters, posters and pamphlets, magazines and books, and as such it constituted a vital part of this emergent counter-public sphere.[2] New things were being said, imagined and discovered. New discourses were being built and contested. Language was being dismantled as a tool of oppression and words as speech, conversation, poetry, information and polemic were reconceived as instruments of liberation. The primary communication technology by which to disseminate this verbosity, as well as its concomitant imagery, was printing. However, for autonomous women's groups espousing unpopular ideas, options in this regard were initially restricted. "Women's Lib" was frequently ridiculed or reviled in mainstream culture — sentiments reflected in the printing trade. Printing was also expensive. The second-hand or loaned stencil-duplicator served a mighty role in this breach, but its capabilities were limited in terms of quantity, quality and format. The women's movement needed a press, or better still, presses, of its own. For feminists to run their own printing presses meant gaining control of the means of production and, crucially, of representation. "We were convinced that

2   See for example Lucy Delap's excellent piece, "Feminist Bookshops, Reading Cultures and the Women's Liberation Movement in Great Britain, c. 1974–2000" in *History Workshop Journal* vol. 81 (2016).

if we were to be heard, if our words were to be published, we would have to control the process of publishing. And for us at that time that meant learning to print" said Sheila Shulman of Onlywomen Press.[3] By the late 1970s, there were a number of entirely female-run feminist printshops dotted over the UK and the arc of their collective existence reflected that of the WLM.[4] In this essay, I sketch out a brief history of what might be called the women's print movement in Britain of this time, from the motivations and the forms it took, to the challenges it faced. The focus here is primarily on the less written about (but more widespread) offset litho printshops rather than the screen-printing poster workshops,[5] although these are certainly part of the story and will be mentioned. I draw on research gathered during my PhD,[6] which grew out of my own involvement in both feminist and "mixed" leftist printshops and a desire to understand more of what I had spent so many years involved with.

3   In "A Press of One's Own", *Trouble & Strife* vol. 26 (Summer 1993), p. 47.
4   For an insightful overview, see Eileen Cadman, Gail Chester and Agnes Pivot, *Rolling Our Own: Women as Printers, Publishers and Distributors*, Minority Press Group, 1981.
5   For an account of the longest-running and best-known of these, see *See Red Women's Workshop: Feminist Posters 1974–1990*, Four Corners, 2016.
6   Jessica Baines, *Democratising Print? The Field and Practices of Radical and Community Printshops in Britain 1968–98*, 2016. Available at http://etheses.lse.ac.uk/3452 ... 52/ [accessed 19 January 2020].

The WLM in Britain began to coalesce in the late 1960s, when small groups of women began forming "consciousness raising" groups and established the London Women's Liberation Workshop. Out of this the magazine *Shrew* was born, which ran fairly regularly between 1969 and 1974, with a few special issues after this time. *Shrew* was produced by different groups of women around the country, who each took charge of a particular edition. How *Shrew* was printed gives an initial insight into the emergence of the feminist printshops. For its first year or so, the magazine was stencil duplicated, then offset-litho printed by various leftist printshops until 1974. In the summer issue of that year, a notice in the magazine proposed a new possibility: "Let's print *Shrew* ourselves next time. A feminist press is forming".[7] It is likely this is the press that became the London-based Women in Print, which started in 1975. At that time, the women who started Onlywomen Press were also undertaking printing training at one of the London colleges and printing feminist materials on the machines there—although not without objections.[8] Onlywomen would finally set up their own printing press in 1978. They were distinctive in that the printing was part of a publishing operation, and most involved were also writers. In the meantime, in 1976, a group of feminists had taken over an existing community printshop in Manchester: Moss Side

7   *Shrew*, Summer 1974, p.6.
8   "A Press of One's Own", op.cit.

Community Press became Moss Side Women's Community Press (also known as Amazon Press). Later, there were other "conversions" such as Bradford Printshop, Open Road in York, Rye Express and for a brief period Islington Community Press, both in London. Ramoth Prints was set up in Nottingham and in 1979 Sheffield Women's Printing Co-op was born. The later issues of *Shrew* could now be, and were, printed by feminist presses, along with other movement materials. During this period, two long-running poster workshops were also established, See Red Women's Workshop (1974) and Lenthall Road Workshop (1975). Most were fulltime operations, making use of cheap space available in dilapidated inner-city areas, and dependent on the free or cheap labour of those involved. By 1977 there were enough feminists involved (or wanting to be) in movement printing and publishing for a national conference, *Womenprint*. This was held at another of the grassroots resources that the WLM had been establishing, Camden Women's Centre in London. It was organised by founders of Onlywomen Press and attended by about 60 women.

The feminist printshops were to an extent part of a larger emergent phenomenon of small radical and/or community printing presses appearing in Britain's cities, such as the above-mentioned Moss Side Community Press. These were set up to meet the communication needs of the more general swell of diverse post-1960s leftist political activity. There were various conditions of possibility that enabled this wider "alternative" printshop scene, not least the opportunity of cheap space mentioned above, but also of particular relevance here, the availability of accessible printing technologies, especially small offset-litho, and for poster making and screen printing. Small offset presses, while using the same technology as the larger offset machines, had been marketed for use in offices as a superior and more flexible alternative to the ubiquitous stencil duplicator. They could be acquired second-hand relatively cheaply and easily, and were to become the bedrock of this alternative printing field, including many of the new women's printshops.

The *Womenprint* conference of 1977 comprised a range of discussions—on feminist propaganda, distribution, skills exchanges, finance, self-publishing, and of course printing. Women from all the above-named presses participated, along with a good number of feminists working within the "mixed" radical and community presses. The notes from the printing workshop are illuminating, and an indication of practices—and refrains—that persisted. Here I want to highlight a particular aspect, organisation and skill within the women's printshops. A line in the report reads, "Although we are aiming to work collectively in a non-hierarchical set-up, it is nonetheless difficult to eliminate patriarchal patterns of learning and teaching, especially when various levels of expertise are involved in both."[9]

9   *Womenprint* report, 1977, p. 1.

Jess Baines

Among other things, this statement reveals a key dimension that was integral to the character of these feminist printshops: they were all collectively run. This way of working was an intrinsic aspect of the WLM—part of its general feminist praxis. A frequent extension of this was the aim that everyone in a group would be able to do/learn everything, or at the very least not be bound to one redundent job or function or part of the process, be that "admin", "design" or "printing". This aim was in one sense pragmatic, to cope with fluctuations of members, but it was also about "skill sharing", another widespread ideal of the WLM. Skill sharing was part of the movement's DIY ethos of breaking down and disseminating knowledge and skills hitherto perceived as "specialist", especially those primarily in the hands of men, from building and gynaecology to printing. Skill sharing and collective self-education was about empowerment—and autonomy. It is notable that the *Womenprint* report states that "everyone who can't print wants to learn". Within a feminist printshop, skill sharing and duplicating roles was also about an anti-hierarchical distribution of knowledge and power. The *Womenprint* report highlights how feminist printshops were often the site of learning how to print in the first place. As we saw with the case of Onlywomen Press, some women did attend printing courses, but these typically involved entering into a sexist male-dominated arena, so the ideal was often for women to teach each other, despite the potential challenges. Many joined without prior skills, although these were always desirable. However, a virtual prerequisite was WLM involvement. Encouraging women to consider printing as a viable job more generally and putting pressure on the printing trade unions was something taken up by feminists, particularly the Women in Printing Trades group formed in the late 1970s, which later also commissioned the educational video, *No Set Type*.[10]

The motivations for joining, rather than setting up, a women's printshop varied, although a frequent theme was to be "doing something" that was part of the women's movement—and to learn to print. Da, who joined Women in Print for example, remembers: "I just thought wow, working with women would be great… and as part of a collective… I joined with no experience… It was like I can learn this and it'll be fun and exciting to learn a whole new skill… It felt like we were very much integral to the women's movement and I think that in lieu of pay there was actually job satisfaction".[11] For other women, as well as being something practical for the movement, the fact that printing was conceived as an arena inaccessible to them meant that it strongly chimed with their feminist politics and identity. Jo, who joined Moss Side Women's Press, recalls: "I was attracted to learning manual trade… Printing was a very male-dominated trade and suddenly it was open

10   Directed by Jane Harris, Wide Angle Productions, 1985.
11   Da Chong, interview with the author, 2011.
12   Jo Somerset, interview with the author, 2011.

to me … it was a collective and all this made it something right for me … The press was part of my activism".[12]

In some sections of the women's movement there was also a certain kudos in being a printer, because it was perceived as breaking gendered roles and capabilities. As Jess from Sheffield Women's Printing Co-op explains, "there was quite a thing about being an A3 printer as well, there weren't many around. People [women] were quite impressed!".[13] This was especially seen to apply to offset litho printing,[14] a more technically complex process than screen-printing—although the commercial screen-printing trade was in fact male-dominated as well. For many women who joined, printing was not a "career choice"—in inverted commas because this kind of future planning was antithetical to the prevailing "structure of feeling" (to borrow Raymond Williams' expression)—but part of broader period of activism and experimentation in their lives. Although some women did spend many years within and across the feminist printshops, or sometimes went to "mixed" radical presses, many more passed through and onto other things unrelated to printing.

The issue of women who had built up skills and then left a press was challenging for the feminist printshops. It often meant more

13   Jess Osborn, interview with the author, 2011.
14   The sense that the small offset printing world was overwhelmingly male is not entirely accurate.

training or skill sharing, which in turn impacted on the quality and quantity of what they could print. Getting sufficient print work to keep going was in itself often a problem. Many of the groups they wanted to work for were on low to zero budgets, and, as explicitly feminist organisations, there were expectations from their women's movement customers to be accommodating. Sliding scales of charges were common. What the feminist printshops could actually print was also restricted by their technology. The largest offset litho press any of them had was A3, not efficient for longer-run magazines or booklets and certainly not books. It was inconceivable for example that any of the presses would have been able to cope with printing the most widely read magazine of the WLM, *Spare Rib*. As such, feminists would end up taking some of their printing to one of the general leftist printshops, which were in some cases relatively sympathetic and often had committed feminists among their workers. A message in the *Womenprint* report by attendees from one of the alternative leftist printshops, Paupers Press in Oxford, is indicative: "The three feminist printers are being starved of feminist material. Any offers??" Although established to support the movement, for the most part there was not enough movement printing of suitable type to sustain the presses. As Moss Side Women's Press stated in 1979, "We couldn't survive on printing women's stuff alone."[15] Work from "acceptable"

15   In *Wires*, an internal WLM newsletter, 1979.

other groups made up the balance, although for this they were in competition with the radical and community presses. Typically, there were policies of sorts about what a feminist printshop would refuse to print; nothing sexist, racist or homophobic were obvious examples. There might also be discussions about whether to print for organised leftist groups such as the Socialist Worker Party, or even individuals.[16] Finally, a significant amount of movement printing continued to be done on stencil duplicators, and in later years on photocopiers, when this became a low-cost option.

The women's printshops described above were born of the 1970s WLM. Like any social movement it was complex and dynamic, comprising many groups and positions, this was reflected in the feminist printshops. The movement was subject to internal flux and contestation and it would perhaps be more accurate to speak of the women's movements of this period—in the plural. However, that which initially defined itself as the WLM was and is a reference, both historically and as a point of critique, as more women found their voice and articulated its failings and omissions.

By the mid 1980s, the movement had changed considerably and some of the grassroots feminist activity that had characterised the 1970s and early 1980s seemed to be waning.

16   Statement by Women in Print, submitted to "How Can Radical Publishing Survive the Eighties?" conference organised by Minority Press Group, London 1980.

Linking her sense of a demise in feminist political activity with changing expectations, Lyser, from Women in Print, recalled: 'It felt like there were fewer issues going on … and it had got all artsy … we just couldn't do what they wanted us to do.'[17] The issue of aesthetics and quality was perhaps also shaped by the inevitable process of new generations of feminists rejecting both the politics and signifiers of their immediate forebears, along with a wider cultural attentiveness to design and style in the 1980s.[18]

The feminist printshops were, for the most part, financially marginal throughout their existence, but they were also part of a women's movement culture that wanted its own presses and saw them as contributing to and prefiguring an alternative feminist reality. They were places where feminists could learn new skills, forge relationships, experiment with anti-hierarchical ways of working, while simultaneously providing a tangible and enabling resource for the women's movement. However, as the efferverscence of grassroots feminism waned, it became ever harder to find women motivated to join the printshops. Feminists were drifting in different directions: working politically with gay men, into "careers", or in therapy and finding themselves. The radical promise of collective working had also taken its toll on many, as well as years of financial precarity. Instant printshops, desktop

17   Lyser, interview with the author, 2011.
18   Angela Phillips. "The Alternative Press", in *The Alternative Media Handbook*, Routledge, 2007.

publishing and photocopying contributed to the decreasing material value of the feminist printshop. (Popular internet access was still to come). There were neither the women nor the viable printing, nor it seems the movement momentum, to sustain the undercapitalised feminist printshops. Onlywomen Press closed early in 1984, Women in Print in 1986, Rye Express in 1987, Moss Side Women's/Amazon Press in 1988, See Red in 1990, Lenthall Road Workshop in 1992, and so on. Other cultural resources of the women's movement also disappeared, such as magazines, bookshops and women's centres. The outlier was Sheffield Women's Printing Co-op, which continued into the early 21st century and which had, unusually, managed to establish itself as the main "alternative" printers in Sheffield.

The confluence of the contemporary revival of feminism and small-scale print culture has resulted in a new interest in the printing activities of earlier feminisms. It could be argued that the extraordinary access to communication provided by digital tools and network technologies mean that there really is no reason for feminists to be printing anything now. And yet. Comparatively, print is a slow and awkward media, a counterpoint to the ubiquity, ease and speed of online material and comment. To print now may in some sense be an act of non-compliance. Print also creates a material culture of tangible, immutable visual objects that act as signs and affirmations of presence, identity and perhaps 'community' —small-scale print especially so.

With thanks to Bishopsgate Archive, Feminist Library (London) and all those I interviewed.

Breaching the Peace, published and printed by Onlywomen Press, 1983. A5 44pp pamphlet: cover design by Cath Jackson. The imprint on the back cover states: "Onlywomen Press is a women's liberation publishing and printing group, producing work by and for women as part of creating a feminist communication network and, ultimately, a feminist revolution".

Jess Baines

the freedom of the press
belongs to those who
control the press.

WOMEN IN PRINT

The Freedom of the Press, from calendar by See Red Women's Workshop, 1978.

Womenprint
Conference 18-19/6/77

Womenprint Conference Report header, 1977.

is a women's liberation publishing and printing group, producing work by and for women as part of creating a feminist communication network and, ultimately, a feminist revolution.

Onlywomen Press, imprint, 1983.
One of the imprints used on the press' own publications since 1979.

printing?

contact:

MOSSIDE
COMMUNITY
PRESS
women's
co-op

21A PRINCESS ROAD, MANCHESTER M14 4TE (061) 226 7115

Publicity poster for Moss Side Women's Community Press, c. 1979.
Courtesy of Bishopsgate Archive.

Sheffield Women's Printing Co-op, logo, 1990.

ROLLING OUR OWN

WOMEN AS PRINTERS, PUBLISHERS AND DISTRIBUTORS

Rolling Our Own (cover), by Eileen Cadman, Gail Chester and Agnes Pivot. Designed by Margo Xeridat, Minority Press Group, 1981.

Shrew (cover), Summer 1978. Issue produced by Women and Nonviolence Study group. Courtesy of Feminist Library, London.

Jess Baines

THE
PUNCTUATION
PETS

An
Apology
to
Grammarians

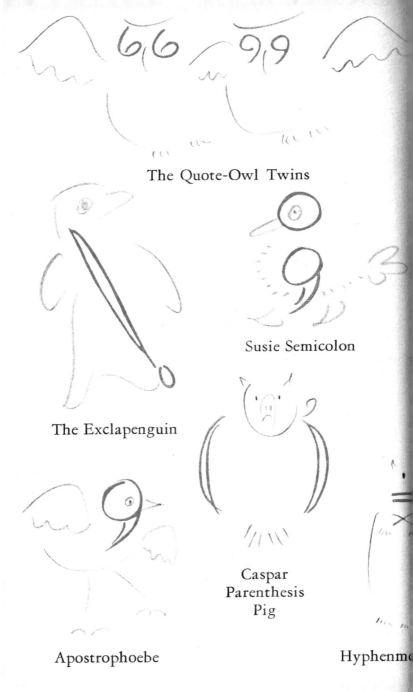

The Quote-Owl Twins

Susie Semicolon

The Exclapenguin

Caspar
Parenthesis
Pig

Apostrophoebe

Hyphenm

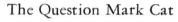

Colonstork

The Question Mark Cat

Otto Dashund

Periodella

Coney the Comma

First Cast in Boredom
January 1936
Redrawn on Scratch Pad
July 1937
Reproduced by
THE MERIDEN GRAVURE COMPANY
Motion Picture Rights Reserved!

The Battle Between

Men and Women in

the Typography Trade

Ulla Wikander

Excerpt from Ulla Wikander,
*Women's work in Europe 1789–1950:
Gender, Power and Division of Labor*,
Atlas, 1999, pp. 80–89.

Excerpt translated from the Swedish
by Kira Josefsson

When printing was a completely new trade in the 16th century, female print workers existed. But relatively soon, through the guild system, men held the sole right to the profession. As an illustration, in 1800 there was not a single female typesetter in London, and it is likely that the situation was the same in other cities and countries. This changed at the end of the 19th century, and a struggle between women and men began. Employers, technology, the right to apprenticeship, union activity, state regulations, and pay levels became tools for both sides to wield. Women wanted the right to work, on their own, but improved terms. Men wanted to exclude women from the printing trade, or at least wanted their work to be regulated in ways the men found suitable. Women were subordinate from the beginning: they were newcomers, intruders.

The problems began when printshop owners started to hire women to meet the needs of a rapidly expanding sector. Women were asking lower pay than men, and therefore printshops were happy to hire them. For women, the pay was still good—their salary as typographers was higher than what they would be paid for other kinds of work. Women performed more or less the same work as men, and they learned fairly quickly. It is possible that they became more specialised, as they weren't given the same training as apprentices, who were all boys. Girls were not accepted into apprenticeship programs. Refusing women education was a method of exclusion.

All over Europe, typographers were articulate and early to organise. The old guilds transformed into powerful and fairly conservative interest groups. Throughout the continent, these organisations laboured to keep women out of their workplaces. They regulated apprenticeship admissions, and would not accept untrained help. Nevertheless, women managed to break into the profession in many countries during the last decades of the century. In France, the number of women in the printing trade doubled between 1866 and 1896, growing from just above 7,000 to almost 16,000. This, however, did not mean that the proportion of women increased; women consistently made up around 20% of the totality of this workforce until 1906. In England, few women worked these jobs; the male unions were more effective in their resistance. Scotland, on the other hand, looked similar to France.

A series of events in Norway's capital Kristiania illustrates the contradictory relations that characterised this old trade, as it slowly became mechanised, along with a halted feminisation, and a newly figured masculinisation. In the 1870s and 1880s, Norway's typographical organisation made efforts to remove women from the printshops. Here, like elsewhere, the organisation enjoyed good relations with the printshop owners. The male typographers tried to get employers on their side in their stance towards female workers. They noted that some printshops engaged in disloyal competition by hiring large numbers of women, who were cheaper. If typographers and employers all agreed to exclude women, both salaries and prices could remain high. Everyone—that is, all men—would benefit. But it was impossible to convince the printshop owners to turn their backs on a new, good and cheap workforce. Male typographers failed in their attempts to create an anti-woman alliance with their employers.

What were the typographers' arguments against women's work? It was said that women would also push down wages for men, that their lack of men's all-round knowledge would make them unprofitable, and that the work would make them ill. Tuberculosis and lead poisoning were common diseases among typographers. Moreover, it was claimed, women's morals would be ruined, and they would not be able to perform their natural duties as wives and mothers. A woman's place was in the home, not at the printing press! But no argument was sufficiently convincing. Printshop owners were unimpressed, and the women remained. Since the debate had played out in public, women were now well aware of the opinions and deeds of their male counterparts.

In a strike for higher pay organised by the male union in 1889, the non-unionised women did not participate. The strike failed, giving the union a costly lesson in the importance of women's voices. They could no longer win a struggle without the women, and they had not been able to get rid of them. The subsequent union strategy was to try to attract women to join the organisation, and in this way keep all wages at a high level. A new attitude was put forth, based on a socialist-inspired analysis—it was not the women's fault that they acted as competitors to the men: they were pitted against the men by capitalism. In fact, women and men were on the same side, in opposition to the printshop owners. Still wary of the earlier dirty tactics of the men, women resisted unionisation, however. Hesitatingly, they agreed to organise during the 1890s. Men continued to hold varying opinions on whether women should do wage work or not.

1896 brought a schism in the union. Without asking the women's opinion, the men demanded shorter hours for women and apprentices. In protest, the female typesetters founded their own sub-committee (Sätterskornas Klubb)—still, however, within the male union. They agreed on a principled statement of equality: "…we ask that the same work hours for male and female typesetters be kept, since a restriction, for example one that prohibits us female typesetters and not the male typesetters from working overtime, would mean greater difficulty for us to find work." The paradox the women were forced into in order to strengthen their labour rights is obvious. They wanted the same hours to not lose their attractiveness as a workforce, but they also wanted to keep their low wages—this, too, to remain competitive. Why should they demand equal pay when they weren't permitted apprenticeship training?

Both women and men had tried to unite with the employers against the sub-group, and here, the women had the upper hand. But the workers were unable to find a strategy that suited everyone. At the core lay the men's refusal to accept women as equal workers, as well as their attitude towards their own unique trade skills, one that was shaped by ideals of masculinity and a monopolised educational strategy.

In 1898, however, men and women for a time succeeded in uniting in a new wage struggle. The female typesetters formulated a demand: they would only participate as long as "the typographers don't work to counter our interests". One of these interests was to maintain lower pay for women, which finally led to the demand to accept women as apprentices. In the long term, this would enable a union demand for equal pay for all.

Male resistance to female workers grew when married women, who sometimes worked for even lower pay than their unmarried colleagues, were hired at the book printshops in increasing numbers at the same time as unemployment was on the rise.

The Norwegian typographers' national organisation responded to the new situation by entering wage negotiations behind the women's backs, demanding immediate equal pay in 1902, and then going on strike with this demand. The women were livid, and entered separate negotiations with the employers, an act the male unions considered strike-breaking. As a result, for many years collaboration between men and women was impossible.

Equal pay has always been a complicated question in the labour market. "Equal pay for equal work" was a demand made at several international congresses in Europe during this period: at women's congresses, and at the Second International. At the same time, large numbers of women working to support themselves and enter the male labour sectors wanted the right to use their wage levels as a competitive edge. What was equality? With whom should you show solidarity? What was class struggle? Should married women not engage in wage work? Should women be given a real education?

During the 1890s and in the early 1900s, a prohibition against night work for women was becoming common in Europe. This caused discord and conflict. The difficulties were evident for typographers, as newspapers are printed at night and overtime was also common at book printshops. Women wanted to keep their comparatively well-paid jobs in these fields, and the prohibition against night work made it difficult.

Separate laws for women, and the prohibition against night work in particular, were discussed both in terms of theory and praxis at international women's congresses, for example at the Congrès Féministe International de Bruxelles in early August 1897. Journalist and magazine editor Maria Martin presented a critique of the French prohibition on night work. Prior to the law's introduction in November 1892, there had been female employees at most printshops, she claimed. After the passing of the law, women were forced to leave several of these shops. Why? The law didn't just regulate night work, but other scheduling as well. After a certain nocturnal hour, employers were required to apply for a dispensation if they wanted to put women on overtime. It was difficult to foresee the need for extra labour, but the formalities had to be taken care of in advance. Many employers, therefore, preferred hiring men, since that required less bureaucracy.

Martin's drastic conclusion, therefore, was that the law was meant to give work to men and ideally ensure that women lost theirs: "Such were the consequences of laws supposed to protect women. It was the labour that was protected, to the benefit of men. The protection of women revealed itself as an oppression."

Norway, of course, also saw female typographers protesting the prohibition against night work as it was about to be passed into law by the Norwegian government just over a decade later, after it had been accepted as an international labour protection convention. At already segregated workplaces like textile factories, a night work prohibition was generally embraced, while women in industrial workplaces with better pay, who worked alongside men, protested. These jobs were not common, so a fairly large number accepted the night work prohibition. It did not apply to the most common female jobs, for example health care or maid work, nor did it regulate jobs in family-owned businesses. The first international labour protective convention of 1906, the Berne Convention, only prohibited women from working at night in factories with fewer than ten employees. The basis of this law was an understanding that women and men belonged to different categories, where one group was able to protect itself through organised labour, while the other was in need of government protection, at the same time as it held special value for the nation state as a potential producer of coming generations.

Laws and unions, then, configured women into a separate and different workforce, while women used all possible means to access better jobs, even when their strategies could be understood as lacking in solidarity with union men. The typographer struggles are of great interest for anybody who wants to understand both the limited participation of women in unions, and men's attitudes to women even *after* they had joined. A very large number of women simply felt persecuted by male-centred union politics, something that evidently hurt the union struggle, but hurt women even more, since it often left them without union support, even when they were members.

A truly bitter contribution to the documentation of what was taking place between women and men was given by French journalist Camille Belilon, at a congress organised by the International Council of Women, in London in 1899. She accused men of *all social classes* of attempting to shut women out of certain jobs. Male union politics were defined by a "misogynistic spirit". In the case of the typographers, she chose the strong word "hatred" to describe the union's attitude towards women. In Belilon's opinion, the separate laws were a result of the union's attempts to eliminate competition. Parliamentary representatives had been manipulated into passing a night work prohibition through appeals to child mortality and the future of the nation—a discourse on motherhood that had caught the lawmakers' ears. Belilon gave her feminist analysis of dependence and independence:

> What is it, to make a woman dependent on a man? Of all injustices, it is the most horrible! Yes, because although the inequality existing between the classes is unfair, it is not more unfair than the one between the sexes, and that injustice is highly immoral, both as such but also because it results in immoral acts. Yes, it is not only an attack on the principle of freedom; it is also to take all power from the woman and give the man all support; it is to put depravity before competence and virtue. To force the woman to ask the man for bread, that is, to introduce prostitution or, what is worse, giving power to the prostitute. We have really had enough of this continuous humiliation.

Women's entrance into the typography trade created a volatile situation with ever-shifting alliances. Tensions boiled over when some typesetters married women who had long worked in the profession. In France, the conflicts between male and female workers can be illustrated by the highly publicised Couriau case, which came to a head in 1913. Emma and Louis Couriau married in 1912 and moved to Lyon. He had been a typographer for 20 years, and was a union man who had participated in activism across France. She had worked as a typographer for 17 years. The Fédération du livre, the national organisation for typesetters, had decided in 1910—after much handwringing and many years of trying to exclude women from the profession—to allow women to join the organisation. The reason was that new mechanical linotypes made women even more attractive hirees. By unionising women, the men hoped for unity in wage negotiations. Just as in Norway, the acceptance of equal pay became a long-term demand.

In Lyon, the Coriaus asked to join the local union. But this large, conservative local chapter refused to include women, and Emma was not permitted to join. Louis was initially accepted, but was expelled when he failed to forbid his wife from working as a typographer. It turned out that the decision by the central union leadership to allow women in the organisation meant nothing in the face of the local chapters to make their own rules.

The Couriau case became a national scandal, with pages upon pages of writing on it, especially in the socialist and anarchist press.

Many union representatives differed in their views from the local Lyon chapter. The debate also engaged bourgeois and socialist feminist groups. The couple enjoyed broad support, and Louis was able to join the national typographical organisation as an individual. In 1914, the war broke out and the story was forgotten. Few improvements of the women's situation occurred after the war, since union organising splintered in France. What could perhaps have been gained from the great public interest in Emma's case paled and disappeared. The long-term result was that men kept, or perhaps more accurately reclaimed, their monopoly on the typography profession.

Material circumstances had been beneficial for women; for typographers, the introduction of typesetting machines had made the work easier than manual typesetting. The growing demand for labour power at the end of the century, together with women's increased general knowledge and their lower wages, contributed to giving them the chance to work as typographers. Ideologically, women's integration into previously male-dominated trades was supported by women's rights' groups and feminists, while the most fervent opposition came from those who ideologically supported a certain idea of the family and the idea of a "natural" gendered division of labour, according to which women and men were not to work in the same professions. This had reverberations for the female wageworker's labour conditions at large, since men—most men—still felt that domestic work was the exclusive domain of women, regardless of whether they were wageworkers or not. One of the male typographers who supported Emma described the women's double-shift in drastic terms:

> If a man is a wage slave, so is the woman. Moreover, she is often the slave of the slave. [...] Even though she works as a man, [...] is affected by the same exhaustion, the same dangers and risks, the woman is paid less. [...] Moreover, when her partner comes home, he expects her to heat up the soup while he smokes his pipe and reads the newspaper. [...] Exposed to a man's influence, his authority, stupidity, and cruelty, the woman is bound— even if she does not want it—to become a mother again and again, and on top of that a housekeeper and lover. [...] Work is the way she can live freely, liberated from the dependence on a man.

This man would have been pleased to see a successful "intrusion" of women into those work sectors understood by men to be their sole domain. If a greater number of female wageworkers had produced a less rigid gendered division of labour, women would have been liberated from the "dependence on a man," and marriage relations, too, would have changed. The debate did not tend to mention the gendered division of labour in the homes, a situation that was rarely questioned. Without help, most women had to take on the increased labour burden that wage work entailed, work in a gender-segregated labour market, and take care of their homes.

*HOW
ONE OF THEM
GOT
THAT WAY*

By Alison W. Davis

*

OF ALL THE WOMEN IN PRINTING I know I am the only one who didn't marry into it or grow into it by way of another job but who knew from Freshman college days what her fate was to be. I remember going around my home town telling inquiring friends and relatives that I was going to be a typographer and giving them the idea I was going to have something to do with maps. I got quite adept at explaining what typography was but I don't think it ever was very clear to any of the neighbors, designing a book being quite unnecessary since books, to them, were something that just grew out of print shops.

I got interested in books through reading them and accidentally beginning to notice their illustrations, binding, and typography, in just that order, over a period of years. During my Freshman year in college I swam into Updike's two volumes and was earnestly excited over the difference between Schwabacher and Fraktur and wangled an admission card to the Morgan Library to see the Gutenberg Bible and be generally paralyzed by the near presence of so many rare items and the so-watchful minions of Belle DaCosta Greene.

I worked on the usual college magazine and in

the spring of my last year started seeking a job in this unfriendly profession. Somehow no one ever recommended any courses such as the ones I now know are given at New York University and by the Employing Printers' Association. There didn't seem to be any ways of getting typographical jobs or experience. The people holding the jobs had just grown into them and were vague and unhelpful about telling me how I could get to be a typographer. Maybe I struck them as vague, too, and probably appeared very deficient in knowledge and experience, which I was. I just had a notion but it was pretty strong.

I went home and mildewed until about Christmas the following year and then one day while reading Paul Johnston's BIBLIOTYPOGRAPHICA, which I had owned for some time, my eye fell on a title page with the imprint "Laboratory Press" on it. That sounded like a school and of the right kind for me. Being at that time in a pretty despairing state I sat down and wrote the Laboratory Press a rather uppety letter about a young woman who wanted very much to be a typographer and no one, particularly the conservatives at Houghton Mifflin and Riverside, would give her the slightest encouragement. That letter happened to strike the master of the Laboratory Press right in the middle of a weakness. He wrote back and told me he'd like to have me as a special student just as one would like to keep a carp in a barrel of

4

fish to keep them all lively—if for no other reason. My letter made him think I might be an
interesting—or at least lively—person and perhaps
the students had been a rather dull bunch that year
without much imagination or any great reverence
for printing from dampened handmade paper.

We got to where we were writing two and three
letters a day and I had started setting type in a
local print shop to learn the case layout and get
some speed in hand composition when Porter Gar-
nett came to New York in March, 1932, to receive
the Graphic Arts medal. We met in Boston and he
liked me as a person but my typographic possibili-
ties were still quite unknown. I think it was my
fitness for the role of carp in the barrel full of
Tech fish that interested Porter rather more than
my ability as a handler of brasses, coppers, and the
famous toilet-paper spaces. And so my seven
months in Pittsburgh were spent unsuccessfully
—and unwillingly—trying to keep out the Pittsburgh "smog" which harassed the mental as well
as the physical vision of the souls of its more sensi-
tive inhabitants.

I took just the one course at Tech and spent
almost every afternoon there setting type, fiddling
with ornaments, and trying to make myself useful.
It must have been a rather poor class that year
because I turned out to be one of its better
students. I became quite good at hand composition
and learned a bit about handling ornaments. I also

5

got pretty good at re-stacking soggy paper that had
been dampened too much. We each set and printed
a couple of specimens. But as for learning how to
lay out a book, cope with the problems of manu-
facturing it, descriptions of processes other than
letterpress, simple facts of binding—to wit, anything useful in learning how to become the manufacturer in a book publishing house, was omitted
from the course. The course was a pleasant and
uplifting experience for the College of Industries
printing student who had spent three years studying the practical side of printing and needed some
polish to finish him off, but I had never had the
practical experience to prepare me for it!

The next winter I went into a job printing plant
to learn something that would be useful to me. But
not before I'd spent a heartbreaking summer of
making calls and writing letters until this five-
dollar-a-week job as a printer's devil looked like a
large leap toward success. I spent a year running
errands, doing odd jobs, finding out that I wasn't
so hot, and getting a little real experience in a few
branches of my chosen profession. Eventually I
decided to become a printing salesman and since
my then boss had no need or desire for new business I moved on to another job plant.

My new boss thought I still needed shop experience and said I would stay "inside" a few weeks
until I understood him and his methods somewhat.
I learned a bitter, back-breaking lot about his

methods. I worked long hours proofreading, feeding the folding machine, saddle-stitching, hand-inserting, collating, padding, wrapping packages and, when not busy, studying papers and type faces. Moreover, I was working for the man who invented the fourteen-hour day. The capitalist's darling ate lunch with the pressmen and began acutely to visualize their outlook on life.

I stood it for seven months because I wasn't going to give up too easily, but actually my health was being affected and so that Saturday I worked all day helping to move into the new plant was my last day, and I went home for a long rest to restore my energy and interest in a new job.

I tried selling printing for three weeks and forever dispelled the illusion that I wanted to be a printing salesman. Then an employment agency got me a job as assistant manufacturer in a publishing house and that is the sad sweet story of how the hell Essie-May got into this business anyway!

But I haven't given you any details like the inside story of letter-spacing at the Laboratory

The constituents referred to fall into three divisions: (1) *Dimensional* (size and proportions): (2) *Tectonic* (plan and construction); and (3) *Visual* (appearance).

Press with tissue paper, and filing commas down to squeeze them into tight lines. Look at the cut of the paragraph on which I spent eight hours trying

to eliminate the tight line. It's from the text of
A FINE BOOK *and has been a fine help to me in my present job.*

And the sad ending is I've never done any designing. Oh, my superior officer says any time I want to take over any of the nuisance jobs I can. But who wants to lift even a languid hand to designate which color in the cheapest grade of cloth to use on the newest of the "inspirational" books? I know the tissue paper spaces and the long hours over the ornament boxes were high comedy but the screaming over the telephone: "For God's sake use any cloth but get us books for the day before yesterday!" is deep tragedy. If you don't mind I think I'll retire to the country and raise Cardigan Welsh Corgis.

Set in 10-point Walbaum and printed by the Stratford Press on cream Albion laid plate finish paper from the Whitaker Paper Company. Linecut from the Eagle Photo Engraving Company.

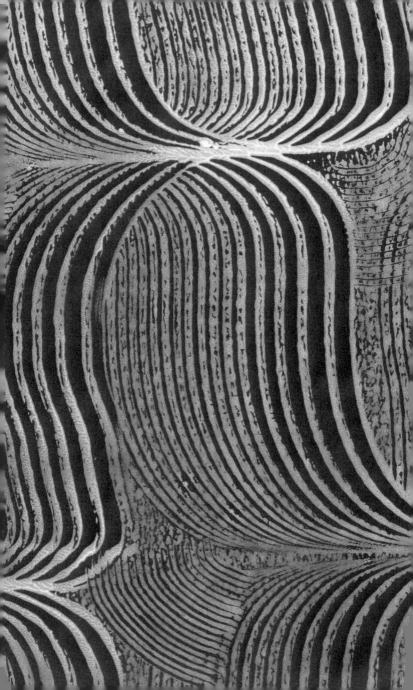

"Even though they might have worked their entire lives in typography as daughters and wives, they are not seen as part of the professional collective."

Excerpt from

a conversation

with Inger Humlesjö

I am still working on my dissertation on the early organising of typogaphers in Sweden, since I've done so much else in the meantime — worked in publishing, as a teacher, and in particular worked with *Häften för kritiska studier* (*Carnets for critical studies*), which we produced in their entirety. But I've remained close to the history of typography and workers. My angle is the history of typographers. It's based on social studies, and studies of family structures. Women have been more or less always present in the typography profession, but they've never been viewed as typographers or as workers or as designers, or taken seriously in any way. This is true for the entire sector, and also for other sectors, with women's entrance into old trades. It's always been difficult. The attitude towards women's contributions has always been that they are lesser. Their work has been devalued. Would it have been devalued if it wasn't known that they were women? That's the question.

What you describe about women not being taken seriously in their professional role remains a common problem. Especially within typography, which is often seen as a trade that only a certain type of man can withstand.

Yes, it's strongly connected to masculinity. Theory around the production of masculinity is one of my starting points. The 1860s and 1870s saw a big discussion in Sweden about what to do with female typographers. Meanwhile, there was a broader acceptance of female typographers in the United States, where they were accepted into unions and were understood to be good at their work. In the US there was a third dimension—race—with black men working as typographers, where the discussion centred on whether they could be seen as real typographers, and this made it easier to accept white women. In the 1880s, typographer union Typografiska föreningen in Stockholm published a journal called *Svensk typograftidning*. It featured reports from congresses in the United States, which describe the race question and how it changed the way female typographers were seen. In Sweden in the 1890s, the woman question became a watershed. Socialists were often in favour of full membership for women, but socialists and liberals had difficulties seeing women as equals, both in relation to the wage question and their standing in other unions.

Is there a particular reason why we should care about typographers today?

They don't exist as a professional group anymore, of course. If you were to walk out and ask someone on the street they'd reply, "Who's that?". If you'd asked the same question in 1985, the reply would have been "They are part of the union struggle". Fria Proteatern produced the theater play *Typerna och draken* (1972), about union struggle in the newspaper world from the 1930s onwards. But today the situation is different. There is no struggle to speak of, and this is connected to the change in the media landscape. Today we primarily consume images. But typographers have done a lot; there are traditions from the typographers that remain meaningful and connected to current developments and the new media landscape.

You could say that one reason to take an interest in typographers is that they were a labour group closer to the written word, which means they were closer to power and a bigger threat to the employer.

You're absolutely right, from the 19th century to 1986. In particular, they thought of themselves as a little better, precisely because they were typographers and literate. In the mid-19th century, conservative typographers were pushing an "orderly" worker's culture, instead of quarrelsome rabble-rousers. They underscored dignity towards and collaboration with the employer, and a keen ear for signals from those in power. They would not have recoiled from collaborating with the monarchy. But in 1870, the liberal wing arrived—it was radical at this time to be a liberal—and questioned this stance. The woman question came at the same time. The old liberals had an ironclad faith in family structures where the man took care of the woman. But there were women in the field, who were seen as nothing. They were servants. They were strongly linked to traditional worker's family structures, where the women also worked. Even though they might have worked their entire lives in typography as daughters and wives, they were not seen as part of the professional collective. In the 1870s, the women became more interesting to employers—they were cheaper, faster, and they didn't cause any problems. This made them a threat to the professional structure in place, and an argument was made that men are the appointed workers and family providers. They needed to have higher wages than women, since women, according to this view, couldn't be providers. They had never heard of single women. There were women who provided for their parents, but they didn't count. The debate was sharpened around the turn of the century, at the same time as loud demands were made to accept them in the unions, otherwise there would be no control over them. The men wanted control over the women, and they also wanted them not to exist—there were a lot of contradictions. In the 1920s, the union Typografiska föreningen created their own employment agency, where they put women in unemployment. Yes, I mean that they did not provide women with jobs, but rather unemployment.

The labour movement has always criticised the liberal labour movement with concepts taken from the 1890s. You have to be really careful to look at the old liberals in relation to their own time period, to see what was new in their look at society in the 1840's. During this time, I would say they were radical, but not in our terms today. But I've gone from the past towards the future, instead of looking back with our current concepts. I've done this in order to understand what the typographers were doing in the 1840's, to find out how they saw themselves. I want to avoid what I'm critical of, which is the labour movement's construction of history.

What is your writing on the construction of masculinity about?

About how this professional know-how is constructed on the basis of a type of masculinity that demands and presents different aspects of the typographer's culture. It's about how they construct themselves. I am pretty critical of the labour movement's historiography. It romanticises the development of the labour movement and its historical radicalism, because it's been dismissive of women and democratic rights. There is a connection between unions and the evolution of the welfare state, the labour movement's idea of what the welfare state should look like and what it should be based on, that men are family providers and women are assistants. It's a history that's lodged deep in our thought and behavior, and through this history we can understand our current society and positions.

"They had to hire lots of women then, who knew how to do this. They were called perforators. They weren't typographers at that time."

Excerpt from

a conversation with

Ingegärd Waaranperä

I worked at publisher Ordfront's printshop. At first it was called U-aktionen and was located in Stockholm. Then, we changed its name to Ordfront [Word Front] and moved to Småland in the South, and I worked there. When we started, around 1969, we were far behind the new technology of the time. Books were made in the cheapest possible way. We went through 200 years of technological evolution in just a few years—it was a chapbook press from the beginning. Our first books were written on a typewriter, with uneven right-hand margins and no kerning or anything. When we moved the printshop back to Stockholm we got an IBM typewriter with a typeball. That was the first embryo of the typesetting shop.

We were basically unpaid. When we arrived in Stockholm with this mode of working, the trade union for printers [Grafiska Fackförbundet] came to us and said, "Hey, you're putting pressure on the market and breaking it for other presses by not charging according to the agreements." We understood this, but we didn't understand how to solve it, so they helped us. We weren't able to negotiate ourselves, since we all acted as employers and employees at once. We had to split up the work force so that some of us got the employer role. We formed a union chapter, started negotiating with each other, and reached minimum wage according to Grafiska Fackförbundet. We had to adjust our prices and finally we conformed to the rest of the sector, and we also got training. The union really helped with our development. They brought us on board, rather than telling us that we were ruining things.

Everyone did everything at Ordfront, but in the end you wound up where you were the best fit, and climbing printing presses was not my forte. I was however the only one who could type at a reasonable speed, and therefore I got that job. It was possible, if you calculated in advance, to get a straight right-hand margin, but we didn't bother. It looked pretty good anyway. But you couldn't make corrections, so if you made a mistake you had to go find that line, write a new one, and paste it on top of the old one. It was a lot of hard work.

We tried different typesetting systems—the job entailed producing long pieces of text. We typeset and printed 70% to 80% of all the left-ist publications in Sweden during the 1970s. We had trouble with line breaks: journals like *Clarté* had narrow columns and you had to fit "Marxism-Leninism" and "the invincible thinking of Mao Zedong". You needed to break the words in the right places, and avoid too much empty space. You can imagine how pissed off we were at these wordy clichés, because they ruined the look of the text.

Later, we moved on to low yellow typewriters where you typed onto a tape, which was read by a computer that directed a little font disc. A strobe inside the disc exposed the relevant letter, projecting it onto light-sensitive paper, so you had to mount the tape in a darkroom. We had bought six different typefaces, and you programmed them while you were writing. It was pretty easy. You brought the galleys to a light table where a stoneman used a machine to smear wax across the back of the paper. Then they'd strip the pieces and place them in templates they had on the light tables. They used thin sheets so they wouldn't have to change the template all the time. This was actually the closest we came to graphic design. The finalised page design was drawn as a dummy reference, and within that, the stoneman could do as he or she wished. But I wasn't so involved in that; I was typing all the time, and I got really fast in the end.

Christer Hellmark worked there as well. We met in 1969 and have been married for 35 years. Christer was behind an expression coined by Ordfront at the end of the 1970s: "the good utility-book". Ordfront's first books were loose sheets glued together in a cold barn in Småland, and as soon as you opened them they fell apart. He got tired of that and pushed the notion that our books should look nice and be usable. Everyone was tinkering in their own way; a slightly bigger text turned into a headline, and so on. Christer started to get interested in graphic design and realised that there were important typographical rules one could relate to. He learned the rules for lead typesetting, all the little square indents and stuff that people thought, "What the h--, why does that matter?". Depending on the machine, we learned different measurement systems. In lead typesetting, there's "cicero" and there are all kinds of fun words that different typographers have for different measuring units.

When you were a member of Grafiska Fackförbundet and were trying to be a good union member, the old men would call you "half-petite" —it was their way of mansplaining. But they were kind and nice, the typographers. It was such a good peer group, really fun people, so self-aware, politically engaged, and radical.

I left Ordfront in the beginning of the 1980s. The only reason being that Christer and I were working at the same place—it became too boring. Grafiska Fackförbundet had their own employment service; when you needed a job, you went to the union first. And they'd say, "They need people at Dagens Nyheter, the newspaper, go there." It was amazing, of course. But that disappeared entirely later.

I came to Dagens Nyheter in 1981 as a "perforator", and they had a system that suited me well. The old linotypes had two keyboards, one for lowercase and one for uppercase. And the old men had been sitting at their linotypes, hammering like this [demonstrates hammering on a keyboard on the table]. They were quick, but when the new machines came they had regular keyboards. They had to hire lots of women, who knew how to do this. They were called perforators, they weren't typographers at that time. There were lots of other differences too, of course, wage gaps and all that. But these old men didn't know this technology. There were a lot of tensions.

We perforators were typing on computers. We were working at the typesetting terminal. The typesetters were the real typographers and of course they were still typographers in the sense that they produced full pages, which we did not. They still had the step of mounting the text on paper, and then they made plates of that for offset printing. When you switched from lead typesetting you also switched to offset printing. Now they could go straight from photo originals to negatives to offset.

At the typesetting shop, when the bosses tried to push us down, for example during wage negotiations, the trade union said "We're in wage negotiations now, so remember that the area around your typesetting machines needs to be very clean." So, at the time, when the newspaper had to get out quickly, we were vacuuming and cleaning our tables and it took forever to get the texts out and the bosses were ready to kill us. It was a tactic: not a strike, but a slowdown.

I worked from 2pm to 10pm. At that hour, we had something wonderful called "homegoing". When everything was finished, backpage ads and everything, the union boss clapped his hands and said, "homegoing". It took 20 seconds for everyone to clear out. We got to go home when we were done with the job, and we were still paid for the entire time. I thought I had died and gone to heaven, because at Ordfront you were never done, and you were never paid.

Ordfront was also very male-dominated. Even though there were women there, the guys had the upper hand. It's only in the last couple of years that feminism has entered publishing. In contrast, the typesetting shop at Dagens Nyheter had many more women. It might have been worse right when the women first entered, because then the older men were afraid of being pushed out—it was their living at stake. But I think the newspaper did it well. They didn't fire people when they changed their technology. A lot of workers had been there for so long that they had lead poisoning, they had sacrificed themselves for the old technology.

The women had the advantage when they came to Dagens Nyheter as perforators, but the struggle was over when I arrived. By then it was a comfortable collective of ladies that welcomed you into their arms. I came right in the middle of the transformation, but it wasn't noticeable at the typesetting terminal shop. When I arrived it was already a pretty female-dominated workplace. Still, the old men did have whisky bottles stashed in their desk drawers. It wouldn't happen that any guys would stalk or touch me; I could tell that time was definitely over. But you could notice it in the lunchroom, not in the sense of sexual harassment, but there were interminable lewd jokes. It was just some of the old men, not that many, but you did choose not to sit at that table in the lunchroom. There were a lot of good people. The struggles that did exist were about professional privileges. Who would own the new technology?

Around 1986, the next restructuring took place. Dagens Nyheter decided to dissolve the typesetting shop, and the journalists were to take over these tasks. This created a big conflict. The typesetters were losing their jobs and journalists had to learn to type and never make mistakes. They were used to filing texts that looked like I don't know what. The first thing that happened when journalists started typing at computers was that their texts became much longer. Before, they had manuscript sheets of 15 lines, half an A4. They were given a request along the lines of "write three sheets" and you did not go over that. But now there wasn't the same concrete limitation, so it went a bit overboard. It's noticeable in the newspapers from around the time. These days, people know how to control themselves.

Typographers fought against journalists doing the typesetting work. But they didn't stand a chance—the whole spirit of the times was that this was the new deal. The typographers were pretty good negotiators, as I remember it. Dagens Nyheter has had much more intense waves of dismissals recently. I was among the first to go, and I said I wanted to join editorial. So I got to start as an editor in the TV section. It was the most low-ranking job, but I wanted to get ahead and I wasn't very old at the time. You still had some potential. Some of the typesetters turned into really good computer technicians. Mostly the men, some of them are now supervisors at the tech unit, or really good graphic designers; they took the chance to develop. The strong sense of honour and pride that typographers had for their profession meant that they were well prepared for the new technology. They were aware of their knowledge, and it did not get lost. They were better equipped than the journalists, because they knew nothing about technology and typesetting. Journalists who were to write in a typographical way needed machines that were pre-programmed to facilitate it.

The entire typesetting unit was integrated into the journalism unit, but when this merger was completed they started to make cuts in the editorial department to fit into the space. They moved out of the skyscraper—from the beginning, all of Dagens Nyheter fit into a big skyscraper with an enormous three-level printer in the basement. They moved the presses to the suburbs, and then they removed the basement, shrank the canteen, integrated the different units in the skyscraper, and finally they were able to squeeze the editorial staff into the building that previously housed Expressen. The entire staff fits on one floor now, except for ancillary units like marketing, which has its own floor. The spirit weakens a little when fewer professional groups are involved. You used to meet and have a lot of discussions across the trades, about design and technology too, not just the content of the texts. Editorial and printing was one unit, standing on the same ground. It was nice.

Grafiska Fackförbundet started as several unions: lithographers, bookbinders, printers, and so on, had their own organisations. Later they were combined, and shrank with time, but they held onto their professional pride and knowledge. They were anti-fascists during the war and have always been a strong force in the defense of free speech. When I think about it, I'm enormously proud to have been part of this professional tradition.

"At the time the technology was overtaking the whole industry and in the union, there was a real struggle between conventional and new technology. We were slow to realise that we would have to embrace unionising and technology."

Excerpt from

a conversation with

Gail Cartmail

Let me tell you a little about my professional background, because it relates to my activism in the National Graphical Association (NGA). Like many of my generation, I left school at 15 with no educational qualifications. The choice for, if I can put it this way, uneducated women was factory, low-level office or the services shops. My parents thought that the best thing would be an apprenticeship, and that sounded wonderful, except the only apprenticeships open to women was in hairdressing. It didn't go well.

Eventually I found a job in publishing selling advertising space. And the young man next to me was doing the same job but was being paid more. I complained to my father and he gave me the best advice anyone could give: "Don't complain, join the trade union and organise". I became active in the trade union, which led me to take on trade union education. I always had an interest in art and eventually I had the opportunity to work in a graphics printshop. Not in graphic design, but more interesting than selling advertising. Equality is such a strong thing throughout our life. You know what I hated the most about the job was not the fact that I was paid less, because I handled that, but the employer's complaints that the only applicants they got were non-white. This is before we had equality laws, before it was illegal to pay a man more and before it was illegal to discriminate blatantly based on skin colour. It was so offensive, and thankfully it is not legal, although it still goes on.

People I knew ran a printshop that published progressive newspapers and magazines and because I was interested in graphic design I started to do artwork voluntarily there. I also worked for a women's collective called Red Lion Setters. The reason I worked there was partly because its connection to the ANC (the African National Congress of South Africa). We did a lot of artwork for the ANC, as well as commercial work. It was nice to donate labour to a movement. Some who were working in the commercial area were using company resources at the workplace at night to do work for non-profit organisations. I have friends who still do the commercial work and then do non-profit work for the community and environmental causes — I think that it is a tradition.

Eventually I became recognised to work in typography and graphics, a very different route compared to an academic or traditional apprenticeship route. And, obviously, I was a union activist, so I became an activist in the print union, the NGA, that actually as a joke was called the "No Girls Allowed" union. But I was young and confident, it would not occur to me that I could be banned. Of course, part-time women workers were not allowed in and that was a great disgrace. It was really obvious that it was necessary for women in the union to work together and also to work with women in other unions in the industries, like the SOGAT (The Society of Graphical and Allied Trades), so we tried to form a network. I think we changed the behaviour and culture. For example, I argued in my chapel for our union, nationally, to be disassociated from the racist South African Typographical Union. And we successfully took that from my workplace through the whole union structures to the international graphic confederation and they were expelled. Actually, guys didn't do that stuff, they did the narrower stuff. We made the argument for the unemployed workers' association and we made the argument for childcare facilities. We scratched our head, "How do you get going the demand for the crèche?" when you don't have that many women in the union and therefore not that many women with children. It's like a vicious circle, isn't it? Finally, we broke through because we formed alliances. And I think we changed some of the language and some respect and I had the fantastic privilege to be the first woman ever elected to represent the union. That was at the TUC (Trade Union Congress) and that was a big thing. It seems so incredible really that those were achievements in the context of what we expect to be normal today. What I know from this is that diversity strengthens organisations, and that includes workers' organisations. And the women made it possible for the union to encourage a much wider diversity including ethnicity and understanding aspects of disability.

A lot of women in the NGA were there because they had QWERTY keyboard skills. Of course, they were intelligent women, so how hard could it be to set type on a computer? I'm not saying it is unskilled work, it is highly skilled. But my belief is that skills attributed to women are not valued as skills until you see them in a male setting. And suddenly everyone is saying, "that's a skill". So, using a QWERTY keyboard competently as well as keeping that within the framework of design, that is a skill.

I was what they called a mother of the chapel, a senior representative. I called the men to a meeting, and if they didn't attend I made them pay a financial penalty. And they attended the meetings. So regularly we spoke together about economic and political issues that were relevant to our workplace, but sometimes bigger than our workplace, like the racism in the South African Typographical Union. The mistake people make is to think that workers have no moral compass and are not interested. My experience is that they are. But we have to create the environment where workers talk to each other in order to understand each other. To understand what is right and wrong, what we have to defend.

I was in the industry up until 1987, and my chapel still had pre-entry closed shop with job list and green card. I always took work that came with the green card and without exception kept them. My chapel was really diverse and we were a strong chapel but already you could see a weakening of confidence in other places. For example, an advertising agency should be trade union and should stamp its artwork with the trade union stamp and then come to us because we did the magazine composition. And in my chapel if we didn't see a stamp, we sent it back, so we held the union line. But because what happened at the time with anti-union laws, the horrendous attack on the trade unions from Margaret Thatcher and coordinated employer campaign, I knew that it was weakening. I know this because our management put more pressure on us to handle non-union work. At the time, the technology was overtaking the whole industry and in the union there was a real struggle between conventional and new technology. We were slow to realise that we would have to embrace unionising and technology. There is a lesson here for us today with automation. The organisation became much poorer, and the least organised area is in the graphic area, partly because it became individualised. Every graphic designer I know is a freelancer; it is not a collective environment. Whereas when I was in the industry we had the originations chapel. Everybody was working as part of a bigger company; the minute you are breaking that up, working for yourself, you become vulnerable. Actually, you are vulnerable workers in so many senses. The strength of the trade union is collective organisation, and the other is decollectivised work.

But we do organise self-employed workers, for example the organisations of self-employed tour guides, organised as union members in a branch where they set the rate and conditions for their work. They are a strong group even as they are in competition with each other, in a way. It's a complex area. It is not typical but in a union of our size we take in small organisations because they can benefit from our services. Recently in the UK artists have formed an organisation, the Artists Union England. Just because it is intellectual creativity in competition with intellectual creativity doesn't mean you don't have common ground and common goals. "An injury to one is an injury to all" is a slogan which I believe is very true. It is in your interest to have bottom a line, a threshold below which you don't go to form an agreement—"this is the rate for the job" and "these are reasonable terms we can negotiate with a client". And form some solidarity so that you are not undercut. And put demands on your clients on how to respect environmental issues. Or an agreement on how not to collude on discriminatory representations. There is an awful lot in your industry where you can have common calls. And I, as a consumer, know that what sets people in this association apart from others is that they might have ethics I can identify with and I feel this can be fair trade. I can see how, with some energy, this can work. Anything's possible.

Nothing is ever achieved by only one person. No employer in my experience has ever given us anything unless we had strength. It is not going to happen if we wish for it. I have achieved nothing individually; it has always been collectively. But what I say to women is that we always give achievements away. And we use the "we" word when sometimes in fact it is individual leadership and we should be proud of leadership roles. Someone has to step up and lead, so my advice is, take strength in your collective but also don't give your achievements away, because that is why women are often not seen as powerful. You know you stand on the shoulders of other women who were also the first women. Once you've broken through, other women will follow. I'm in this fantastic position of just being able to say "you know I'm going to pick women". So, actually, that is what I do, I pick women. I know you will also be in the position and that is the way we are going to change the world.

"Typesetting became typing rather than putting 26 lead soldiers together."

Excerpt from

a conversation with

Megan Dobney

I went to London College of Printing and did a three-year course in typographic design. When I came out of that in 1972, I got a job in a small design studio as a junior designer. At around that time, the print unions were just beginning to see the "technology changing". Before it had been about "we men with our heavy metal" and the "girls out there typing". But, when the technology changed, typesetting was being done on QWERTY keyboard rather than old linotype keyboard. Typesetting became typing rather than putting 26 lead soldiers together.

And in Britain by the 1970s it was women who were typists, not men, so if there was an opening for a typist it would be a woman who went for it, generally speaking. What was happening of course was that girls typing don't cost that much when compared to men with five years of apprenticeships, so there was a concern that the jobs would start drifting into the non-union sector.

There was an expression: "dilutees". Diluting the terms of conditions, but this of course was all about the employers. It was the employer who saw an opportunity to break the hold of the union in terms of wages and conditions. And the response from the union was "we are not having any of it, if you are a woman and work here you get the same wage as I do". You know, within a trade union shop. So they gradually accommodated this.

At that time we had a "closed shop" system in the printing industry, which means that you had to be a trade union member to get a job. So what they decided was that they would open up union membership to people working in this new technology sector. The two unions which were really relevant were the NGA (the National Graphical Association) and SLADE, which later became a part of the NGA.

SLADE was the Society of Lithographic Artists Designers Engravers and Process Workers. They basically did filmmaking, in some of the old school places they did lithography, but not printing presses as such. It was a pre-press process, as composing was in the NGA. But the new technology was relevant to both unions. Whereas there were much clearer demarcations in the old technology, the new technology created more fluidity. NGA and SLADE had a bit of a war for membership and opened up for members who had not done apprenticeships.

There were some interesting times in the early 1980s when there were a few women who set up cooperatives. Mostly typesetters but also printers, producing small prints, leaflets, booklets rather than newspapers. That caused the union some difficulties because they always retained control over employment. If an employer wanted a typesetter they would inform the union and the union would send someone along. Of course that had a massive benefit in one respect. I could walk into a job and because I didn't look like a bloke you'd be welcomed with "Are you sure you can do this?". Then you would show your union card and since they couldn't send people away who could do the job, they would say "Alright we give you a fortnight's trial".

We couldn't be told we were not suitable without the fortnight trial —and of course we were always suitable. But some of these women's printshops only wanted female workers. If they had a vacancy, the union would take the top person on the list who would be a man, of course, because it was a male-dominated industry. So there were some interesting discussions on how they could work around this without giving up the closed shop and the control of everything.

I was very involved in the union so I always felt I had comradeship around me. It wasn't necessarily in relation to the workplace, but as union colleagues. Maybe my memory is fading but I can't think of an evil time with colleagues. Employers, generally speaking, didn't bother, they were not interested in gender really. The only time it became an issue was when you started to have children. When I had mine we

NGA banner in Megan Dobney's office, 2017
Photograph: Sara Kaaman

didn't have that many rights. We don't have that much better rights today in terms of time off and so on.

There is also some protectionism as well. The Luddites in Britain opposed the bringing in of industrial machines because employers used it as an opportunity to reduce employees' wages, power and conditions. But it was progress as well. So it is about making progress whilst retaining control, which is not always easy.

Technology has always changed. But how do you keep control, while introducing this new technique that could possibly provide you with better conditions? A faster printing press is the same basic technology but one that operates more quickly. What trade unions normally try to do is to harvest some of the benefits, so that it does not all go to the employer.

When the employer says we are bringing in a new machine, the union would say, "OK, at what rate would it produce more within a given time frame? Will it be better of quality? Will it require different kind of work? Would you have to run more or whatever?"

And then you take some of that, by saying "We will have more money for it" or "We have another three days of holidays" or "half an hour of the week" but you always try to take something, because otherwise it all goes to the employer and it is not only the employer who is investing. The workforce has to invest in it too, otherwise it doesn't function.

We had complained that we wanted a women's committee for quite a while. But it was when the NGA merged with NUWDAT (the

National Union of Wallcoverings, Decorative & Allied Trades), in 1981 or 1982, that it happened. There were quite a lot of women in their membership, particularly in the design and admin part of these factories. They had a bit of a history of recognising that women needed a bit of space on occasion, so when they came in with us that pushed it quite a bit. I think it was called an "advisory committee" to make sure we wouldn't run away with any idea of power. And it was chaired by a member of the national council who was of course a man, which they all were.

After the Wapping dispute in 1985–86, there was a call at a London conference for there to be an LGBT-committee in the union. Or no, I don't think the T was there then, the LGB-committee, and it was fascinating because on the one hand blokes were saying "They would be wanting a one-legged sailor committee next", but on the other you had the workers of Wapping who said "They were there every Saturday with us", since there had been a support group called "Lesbian and Gays Support the Printers", during the strike.

In those days, and maybe still today (but I don't know anything about it), there was an international print confederation. One of the things that came out of it was that if you were working in Sweden and were a member of the Swedish print union you were a member of the international. You could come along with your membership card to my union office and say "I'd like to work in London" and they would say "OK fine, sign up", and I could do the same in Sweden. One of the outcomes of that was that there was quite a high proportion of black printers who came over from former colonies, from Jamaica and West Indian Islands, including women. It seemed to me that the printing community was a little bit more gender mixed.

The attendees at the 1981 NGA FoC's course. FoC means Father of the Chapel; I was of course an MoC, Mother of the Chapel, but as you can see there weren't many women on it!

Megan Dobney and Arthur Scargill, at the time of the Miners' Strike of 1984–85.
"Print workers raised enormous sums of money to support the striking miners and their families and I went, along with members from the *News of the World* Chapels, to meet Arthur Scargill, then general secretary of the National Union of Miners, to bring cheques and this commemorative piece of propaganda!"

Megan Dobney

Entry into the industry before the technological change was mostly through father-to-son apprenticeships and it was unusual for daughters to take apprenticeships. And obviously they were all white and their sons were white.

Another thing I was very involved in was that we were arguing for the expulsion of the South African Typographical Union from the International Graphical Federation, during the time of apartheid. We said they were not fit to be members of an international trade union, because of their discrimination. They carried out the apartheid themselves as the membership was white, and they didn't have black members and so on. So we took up some of the wider issues. You saw from the miner strike that millions of pounds came in from here and there, from unions all over the world. The same happened during the Wapping dispute.

Thatcher was elected in 1979 and over the next 5–6 years she presented a series of laws that bit by bit cut the rights of the trade unions. Key for the printing industry was the abolition of the closed shops. It was made unlawful to say you had to be a union member before you could get a job. That had a large impact. The unions were not used to recruiting people because everybody knew you had to join the union to get a job at some point. I didn't have to persuade you how good it would be for you to join the union, which is what unions have to do today. At the same time we faced increased globalisation, which had nothing to do with Thatcher in that sense, but print jobs were being sent off to India in the early days or the Philippines, where it was cheaper or investments in new technology were made.

So you could not rely on your work as a designer or my work as a typographer ending up in a British printshop. Before you had to send the film over; now it went straight from a computer to a plate in New Delhi. A lot of things happened that undermined our strength.

I always think of it as a time of great comradeship through the union, in trying to change things. There was some really good support. And we had some pretty decent wages compared to other jobs. It is not so clear-cut now but certainly then, if you had a degree, you would get a better paid job than if you didn't have a degree. Now there are more people with degrees so that premium is diminishing.

But for someone like me without a degree, it led to a job that was well paid. When I was working nights at an ad-setting house, it was fantastically well paid compared to anybody I knew. You know, four nights a week, and if I worked a fifth night, which I did on occasions, it was the equivalent of half a week's pay in addition. Because the structure of overtime was really clear and not "just hang on and do a bit more", but more "that's it, I'm going" or "I'll do another round of work", and then you were going to be paid for it. Very straightforward, and that is a good lesson for any work. You are not here to help out the governor.

I'm not really a scholar, but it may be said that the unions were not nimble enough. Perhaps they rested too much on the control they always had without seeing the future, where it could be different.

Are Women the Natural Enemies of Books?

WRITTEN BY ANNE LYON HAIGHT

ILLUSTRATED BY ANNE HEYNEMAN

DESIGNED BY LEONTINE GENSAMER

PRINTED AT THE POWGEN PRESS

Are Women the Natural Enemies of Books?

In my search for knowledge about lady bibliophiles I climbed the library ladder and among the books on collecting saw "The Library", by Andrew Lang, London, 1881. Confident that I would find some charming and sympathetic essay on the subject, I took it down and turned to the index, but evidently I had forgotten Lang's prejudice, for to my horror the startling lines "Women the natural foes of books" met my eye. They were classed with the other enemies of books; damp, dust, dirt, book worms, careless readers, borrowers, book stealers, book-ghouls, etc. so I hastily turned to the page and read: "Almost all women are the inveterate foes, not of novels, of course, nor peerages and popular volumes of history, but of books worthy of the name. It is true that Isabelle d'Este and Madame de Pompadour and Madame de Maintenon, were collectors; and, doubtless, there are many other brilliant exceptions to a general rule. But broadly speaking, women detest the books which the collector desires and admires. First, they don't understand them; second, they are jealous of their mysterious charms; third, books cost money, and it really is a hard thing for a lady to see money expended on what seems a dingy old binding, or yellow paper scored with crabbed characters. Thus ladies wage a skirmishing war against booksellers' catalogues, and history speaks of husbands who have had to practise the guile of smugglers when they conveyed a new purchase across their own frontier. Thus many married men are reduced to collecting Elzivers, which go readily into the pocket for you cannot smuggle a folio volume easily."

Poor man, his experience with the fair sex must have been a very unfortunate one. Perhaps he had been disillusioned by reading of the sixteenth century abbess of the convent of Rumsey in Hampshire, whom Dibdin tells about. She was bibulously rather than bibliographically inclined and bartered the books of the abbey for strong liquors and consequently was accused of immoderate drinking, especially in the night time when she invited the nuns to her chamber to participate in these excesses. But fortunately the women whom Lang describes in his diatribe are really the rare exception to the rule and only lack of space prevents my writing a folio volume about the many famous women collectors who have been friends not foes to books throughout the ages.

It is true though that the female of our species has never been as susceptible to the malady of book madness as the male, possibly because she has not had the same opportunity. Unless a woman is economically independent there are many demands upon her allowance and consequently she must really want a book very much to buy it instead of a new hat or something else that is dear to her heart. She is not as apt to buy for speculation or because a book is one of the conventional collector's items, but is more independent and adventurous in following her personal taste, although the spirit of a true collector of books is the same whether it be possessed by man or woman.

Strange to say, the first bibliophile on record is a woman. She was a Benedictine abbess named Hrotsvitha who lived in Saxony in the tenth century, and not only had books written for her convent, but wrote plays and translated Terence. Her example was followed in the next century by the lovely and intelligent Countess Judith of Flanders, who, wherever she followed her warring English husband caused the most exquisite illuminated manuscripts to be made. She continued her interests on the continent when she later married the Duke of Bavaria. Four of her manuscripts, magnificently bound, are now safely housed in The Pierpont Morgan Library where "though they are books worthy of the name" their beauty may be appreciated by women who are not even "the brilliant exception to the general rule" of collectors.

The Golden Age of women bibliophiles in France from the fifteenth through the eighteenth centuries must have been a glorious time to have lived. The Queens, the Princesses, the Mistresses of the Kings and all the great ladies had their libraries. They were composed of beautifully illuminated breviaries, missals and manuscripts and from the presses of the great printers of the day came romances, histories, plays and religious books, veritable works of art. These books and manuscripts were bound in gold and silver and jewels, embroidered velvet, and in some of the most beautiful leather bindings the world has ever seen. Briefly; Marguerite of Navarre was one of the famous scholars of her day and the author of a collection of love stories, "The Heptameron." It is said of her "L'amour du livre, chez la fille de Catherine fut une véritable passion". Her books were bound by the famous Clovis and Nicolas Eve and were decorated with daisies. Madame de Pompadour was for many years an inspiring influence in art and letters, although she owned more plays, novels, and other "productions légères" than serious works. She had a printing press at Versailles and also etched plates for illustrations and as gifts for her friends. La Countesse de Verrue was a discriminating collector, a patroness of all the arts and a fascinating woman. The Du Barry acquired 1,068 volumes. When she began to form her library she could scarcely read or write. However, with practise, she soon learned to read well, but like many of us never to spell. Anne of Austria was fortunate in having her friend Mazarin, a kindred spirit in bibliomania, to advise her. Marie Antoinette had two libraries. She kept her particular books in her boudoir in the

Trianon and the titles in the catalogue are very entertaining. Marie Stuart had a catholic taste in literature and her books were exceptionally well chosen. In deference to the loss of her first husband some were bound in black with black edges. It is comforting to know that when she left France as

a young widow to return to her native Scotland where so much tragedy awaited her "qu'elle avait pour les livres un goût profond, et ils etaient pour ainsi dire sa seule consolation loin de ce beau Pays de France." In England, one of the most fortunate of the many ladies who appreciated literature was Queen Elizabeth, for she lived in an age when masterpieces were being written, many of them dedicated to her and many inspired by her. When she was young she embroidered velvets in gold and silver threads to bind her treasures. Among the manuscripts in the Bodleian Library are the "Epistles of St. Paul, etc." which was Elizabeth's own book. She has written at the beginning "I walke many times into the pleasant fields of the Holy Scriptures, where I plucke up the goodlie-some herbes of sentences by pruning: chaw them by musing: and laie them up at length in the hie seate of memorie by gathering them together: that so having tasted their sweetness I may the less perceave the bitterness of this miserable life."

One of the most touching and beautiful tributes ever written to a woman is Sir Philip Sidney's dedication of his "Arcadia" to his "deare ladie and sister", the Countess of Pembroke to whom he wrote in part; "you desired me to do it, and your desire, to my hart is an absolute commandment. Now it is done onelie for you, onely to you." She was his great inspiration and helped him in the editing of the book.

Where there's a will there's a way and women seem able to smuggle folios as well as duodecimos into the library. Catherine de Medici, for instance, had such a passion for books that she got them by fair means or foul. She longed for the library of her cousin Marshal Strozzi and as soon as he died appropriated it for her own. Catherine neglected to pay for it and owed the booksellers as well, so after her death when her books were about to be seized by her creditors, De Thou raised the money to pay for them and they were saved for the state. The fascinating and glamorous Diane de Poitiers was a practical business executive as well as a bibliophile, for it was she who supposedly advised Henry ii to pass an ordinance requiring publishers to present a copy of each book they published to the royal libraries at Blois and Fontainbleau thereby increasing these collections by more than seven hundred volumes. Thus the present day copyright law was initiated by a woman. Catherine of Russia was also courageous in her methods of gratifying her literary tastes. She partitioned Poland in 1772 and seized enough books to form the foundation of the Imperial Library at the Hermitage. She used to ask the Ambassadors, particularly the Ambassador from England, to get foreign books for her and if she did not have the money to pay for them at the time she conveniently forgot about it.

In later days there were women in the young colony in America who enjoyed their books in the midst of their primitive surroundings. In 1643 in Emans, New York, the inventory of the Widow Bronck included Danish books. Mrs. Willoughby of Virginia left over one hundred volumes at her death in 1673 and in 1700 Elizabeth Tatham of New Jersey left five hundred and fifty-two volumes, while their New England contemporary, Hannah Sutton, acquired a library of about seventeen hundred volumes.

In the early nineteenth century Miss Richardson Currer of Eshton Hall, Craven, Yorkshire amassed a large and scholarly collection of books on many subjects. It was housed in a great room with a gallery which must have been the envy of all booklovers. She was the

fond possessor of the rare "Book of St. Albans" written and compiled by Juliana Berners, prioress of the nunnery of Sopwith in Hertfordshire. It is said that the ardent book collector Richard Heber, being unable to secure the book in any other way ardently proposed marriage to Miss Currer. She was firm in her refusal however, preferring to keep this first book about sport to be written by a woman to herself.

One of the most learned lady bibliophiles of this century in America was Miss Amy Lowell of Cambridge, Massachusetts. Her books and manuscripts, including her collection of Keats, are being preserved for posterity in the Harry Elkins Widener Memorial at Harvard. She always enjoyed smoking a good cigar while writing or carrying on her sparkling conversations as she thought it made her thoughts flow more easily.

One could not write of women in connection with books without speaking of two distinguished custodians of famous libraries, scholars, who are as well known abroad as in America; Miss Belle Da Costa Greene, the brilliant Director of The Pierpont Morgan Library, and Miss Ruth Sheppard Granniss, the Librarian of The Grolier Club and sympathetic friend of all bibliophiles, male or female. They, of course, come under Lang's category of exceptional examples.

But what of the many other exceptions?

Would Lang have thought that Miss Lowell could not understand books? or that Diane de Poitiers could be jealous of their mysterious charms? or that Catherine of Russia would hesitate to spend what money she could procure to satisfy her passion for them? What could his lady friends have been like to be classed with the enemies of books—and such enemies at that?

It would appear that book collecting is a truly feminine pastime, containing many elements which appeal to their sex; romance, intellectual curiosity, love of the beautiful and the quest of something difficult to obtain. But feminine collectors should beware of pitfalls, for sometimes this mania arouses the baser instincts such as envy, extravagance, and self-indulgence. Wives have even been known to spend their marketing money on books instead of daily bread and to waste hours reading book catalogues instead of attending to their housewifely duties. Book collecting, however is a common denominator of all ages and a medium through which the minds of both sexes may meet with pleasure and therefore greatly to be recommended as a delightful occupation.

Biographies

Jess Baines holds a PhD from London School of Economics (LSE) on the history of late 20th-century radical printing workshops, and an MA in 20th-century Art History & Theory (2003) from Goldsmiths College, University of London. Since 2003 she has been a lecturer in the Faculty of Design at London College of Communications (LCC). Baines worked as a printer in various radical printing collectives over a period of 12 years.

Ida Börjel is a poet and translator based in Malmö, Sweden. Her debut book of poetry *Sond* was published in 2004. Börjel's work has been translated into 21 languages. Börjel has translated into Swedish work by Solmaz Sharif (together with Jennifer Hayashida), and in her travels in the Middle East she has translated Samira Negrouche, Dahlia Taha, and Mona Saffar.

Gail Cartmail is Assistant General Secretary at the trade union Unite in the UK. Cartmail worked in the printing and publishing industry in the 1970s and 1980s, and studied graphic design and layout at the London College of Printing. She first joined the union in 1975 and eventually became Mother of the Chapel for the print union, the National Graphical Association, where she campaigned for equal pay for women.

Megan Dobney served as the Regional Secretary of the Southern and Eastern Regional Council of the Trades Union Congress (SERTUC) in the UK. between 2007 and 2018, before retiring. She started her activism as a print worker and member of the NGA, National Graphical Association. In recent years she has been campaigning for a permanent statue of suffragette and socialist activist Sylvia Pankhurst on Clerkenwell Green in London.

Eller med a is a graphic design and publication studio located in Copenhagen and Oslo, consisting of graphic designers **Lotte Grønneberg**, **Marte Meling Enoksen** and **Karen Grønneberg**.

Inger Humlesjö was an editor and doctoral candidate in Economic History at Uppsala University, Sweden. Her dissertation-in-progress focuses on the unionisation of typographers in Sweden and the masculinisation of workers' history. Since 1968, she has edited and published the independent socialist journal *Häften för kritiska studier* (*Carnets for Critical Studies*) together with her partner Göran Fredriksson.

Maryam Fanni, **Matilda Flodmark** and **Sara Kaaman** have been collaborating since 2012 under the moniker **MMS** on investigations and writings related to visual culture, with a focus on feminism and workers' history.

Kathleen Walkup is Trefethen Professor of Book Art at Mills College in Oakland, California, where she teaches typography and letterpress printing, artists' bookmaking and seminar courses that combine print culture and book history with studio projects. Her research interests include the history of women in print culture and conceptual practice in artists' books. In the 1970s, she was a partner in Five Trees Press in San Francisco, where she founded the first women's letterpress job shop in that city since the 19th century.

Ingegärd Waaranperä is a culture journalist and theatre critic based in Stockholm. She was a typographer at the magazine and publisher Ordfront between 1972 and 1980 and at the daily newspaper *Dagens Nyheter* between 1980 and 1983 before she became an editor and critic. Today she is a freelance journalist and a critical voice regarding working conditions and cuts in the cultural sector.

Ulla Wikander is Professor emerita at the Department of Economic History at Stockholm University. Her 1977 dissertation was on Ivar Kreuger's match monopolies. Since the 1980s, her focus has been on working life from a gender perspective. Her book *Kvinnoarbete i Europa* (*Women's Work in Europe*) from 1999 chronicles the effects of industrialisation and democratisation on women's wages and work.

Further Reading

In English

Becker, Beatrice Lamberton. (1981).
A Printers' Widow.

Cadman, Eileen, Chester, Gail, Pivot, Agnes. (1981).
Rolling Our Own. London, Minority Press-Group.

Cockburn, Cynthia. (1991). *Brothers: Male
Dominance and Technological Change*. New ed.
London: Pluto Press.

Deakin, Phyllis A. (1984). *Press On*. Women's
Press Club of London, H.E. Walter.

Grabhorn, Jane Bissell, & Teiser, Ruth. (1966).
The Colt Press. Berkeley, University of California.

Hayton, Annette. (1995). *Women, Work and New
Technology: The Case of Desktop Publishing:
Implications for Education and Training*, University
of London Post Sixteen Education Centre.

No Set Type. (1985). Women in Printing Trades.

Oldfield, Otis. (1968). *The Compleat Jane Grabhorn:
a Hodge-podge of Typographic Ephemera, Three
Complete Books, Broadsides, Invitations: Greetings,
Place cards, &c., &c*. San Francisco, Grabhorn-
Hoyem.

Sands, Jennifer. (2010). *Jane Grabhorn:
A Professional Biography of a Woman Printer*.
M.A. thesis, Arizona State University.

Stein, Gertrude, et al. (1937). *Bookmaking on the
Distaff Side,* New York, Distaff Side.

På svenska

Ekdahl, Lars. (1983). *Arbete mot kapital —
Typografer och ny teknik — Studier av Stockholms
tryckeriindustri under det industriella genombrottet*,
Lund, Studentlitteratur.

Humlesjö, Inger. (1998). Manlighetskonstruktion
i arbetarhistoria och fackföreningar. *Häften
för kritiska studier*. 1998 (31):3, s. 3–13.

Johansson, Elin. (1939). *Typografiska kvinno-
klubben 1904–1939*. Stockholm: Typografiska
föreningen.

Lundin, Susanne. (1992). *En liten skara äro vi-:
en studie av typografer vid 1900-talets första
decennier*, Stockholm, Carlsson.

Rehnberg, Mats. (1952). *Typografminnen*,
Stockholm, Nordiska museet.

Wikander, Ulla. (2006). *Feminism, familj och med-
borgarskap: debatter på internationella kongresser
om nattarbetsförbud för kvinnor 1889–1919*.
Göteborg: Makadam.

Wikander, Ulla. (2006). *Kvinnoarbete i Europa
1789–1950: genus, makt och arbetsdelning*.
[Ny utg.] Stockholm: Atlas.

Thank you

Göran Fredriksson, partner of Inger Humlesjö,
for his invaluable help in editing the interview with
Inger as well as being an important conversation
partner for us along the way; Ann Field, archivist
and librarian at the Marx Memorial Library in
London, for her generous help in providing us with
research material and introducing us to former
printers Megan Dobney and Gail Cartmail; Heather
Jardine and Penny Dynan at the St Bride Foundation
Library for retrieving books for us; graphic artist
Ulla Wennberg for her great support, and for
generously sharing her knowledge of printmaking
and the dear moments in her amazing studio;
director of Kretsen Södertälje Olof Sandahl for
sharing his expertise in typesetting and for his
genuine engagement in our project; director
of Grafikens hus Nina Beckmann for believing
in our project, supporting us with an artist-in-residency
and introducing us to Olof Sandahl; artist Ciara
Phillips for the playful and inspiring screen-printing
workshop at Konsthall C; graphic artist Emmy Dijkstra
for teaching us the fascinating technique of paper
lithography; bookbinder Katja Winkes at Leksands
folkhögskola for guiding us through the process
of paper marbling; director of Konstakademien
(Royal Swedish Academy of Fine Arts) Elisabeth
Alsheimer Evenstedt; technician Fritz Quasthoff
and assistant Jennifer Bergkvist in helping us arrange
the exhibition. Last but not least a huge thank
you to all the contributing writers and interviewees
for their patience and all their efforts to make this
book possible.

LEISURE

What is this life if, full of care,
We have no time to stand and stare;

No time to stand beneath the boughs
And stare as long as sheep or cows;

No time to see, when woods we pass,
Where squirrels hide their nuts in grass;

No time to see, in broad daylight,
Streams full of stars, like skies at night;

No time to turn at Beauty's glance,
And watch her feet, how they can dance;

No time to wait till her mouth can
Enrich that smile her eyes began?

A poor life this if, full of care,
We have no time to stand and stare!

Natural Enemies of Books
Edited by Maryam Fanni, Matilda Flodmark, Sara Kaaman

Essays by Maryam Fanni, Matilda Flodmark, Sara Kaaman,
Kathleen Walkup, Ida Börjel, Jess Baines, Ulla Wikander

Copy-edited by Antony Hudek, Sarah Horn
Translation by Kira Josefsson

Published by Occasional Papers

Graphic design by Eller med a
Typeface   Arial (Robin Nicholas, Patricia Saunders)
              Filosofia (Zuzana Ličko)
Printed by TMG Stockholm

Supported by The Swedish Arts Grants Committee

All images © 2020 the contributors or their estates

Occasional Papers
occasionalpapers.org

ISBN 978-0-9954730-3-4

K | THE SWEDISH ARTS GRANTS COMMITTEE